STAAR

Grade 4 Reading Assessment

SECRETS

Study Guide
Your Key to Exam Success

STAAR Test Review for the
State of Texas Assessments
of Academic Readiness

Dear Future Exam Success Story:

First of all, **THANK YOU** for purchasing Mometrix study materials!

Second, congratulations! You are one of the few determined test-takers who are committed to doing whatever it takes to excel on your exam. **You have come to the right place.** We developed these study materials with one goal in mind: to deliver you the information you need in a format that's concise and easy to use.

In addition to optimizing your guide for the content of the test, we've outlined our recommended steps for breaking down the preparation process into small, attainable goals so you can make sure you stay on track.

We've also analyzed the entire test-taking process, identifying the most common pitfalls and showing how you can overcome them and be ready for any curveball the test throws you.

Standardized testing is one of the biggest obstacles on your road to success, which only increases the importance of doing well in the high-pressure, high-stakes environment of test day. Your results on this test could have a significant impact on your future, and this guide provides the information and practical advice to help you achieve your full potential on test day.

Your success is our success

We would love to hear from you! If you would like to share the story of your exam success or if you have any questions or comments in regard to our products, please contact us at **800-673-8175** or **support@mometrix.com**.

Thanks again for your business and we wish you continued success!

Sincerely,
The Mometrix Test Preparation Team

Need more help? Check out our flashcards at: http://MometrixFlashcards.com/STAAR

TABLE OF CONTENTS

INTRODUCTION **1**

SECRET KEY #1 – PLAN BIG, STUDY SMALL **2**
INFORMATION ORGANIZATION 2
TIME MANAGEMENT 2
STUDY ENVIRONMENT 2

SECRET KEY #2 – MAKE YOUR STUDYING COUNT **3**
RETENTION 3
MODALITY 3

SECRET KEY #3 – PRACTICE THE RIGHT WAY **4**
PRACTICE TEST STRATEGY 5

SECRET KEY #4 – PACE YOURSELF **6**

SECRET KEY #5 – HAVE A PLAN FOR GUESSING **7**
WHEN TO START THE GUESSING PROCESS 7
HOW TO NARROW DOWN THE CHOICES 8
WHICH ANSWER TO CHOOSE 9

TEST-TAKING STRATEGIES **10**
QUESTION STRATEGIES 10
ANSWER CHOICE STRATEGIES 11
GENERAL STRATEGIES 12
FINAL NOTES 13

READING ASSESSMENT **15**

READING PRACTICE TEST #1 .... **31**
PRACTICE QUESTIONS 31
ANSWERS AND EXPLANATIONS 43

READING PRACTICE TEST #2 .... **48**
PRACTICE QUESTIONS 48
ANSWERS AND EXPLANATIONS 58

HOW TO OVERCOME TEST ANXIETY **62**
CAUSES OF TEST ANXIETY 62
ELEMENTS OF TEST ANXIETY 63
EFFECTS OF TEST ANXIETY 63
PHYSICAL STEPS FOR BEATING TEST ANXIETY 64
MENTAL STEPS FOR BEATING TEST ANXIETY 65
STUDY STRATEGY 66
TEST TIPS 68
IMPORTANT QUALIFICATION 69

THANK YOU **70**

ADDITIONAL BONUS MATERIAL **71**

Introduction

Thank you for purchasing this resource! You have made the choice to prepare yourself for a test that could have a huge impact on your future, and this guide is designed to help you be fully ready for test day. Obviously, it's important to have a solid understanding of the test material, but you also need to be prepared for the unique environment and stressors of the test, so that you can perform to the best of your abilities.

For this purpose, the first section that appears in this guide is the **Secret Keys**. We've devoted countless hours to meticulously researching what works and what doesn't, and we've boiled down our findings to the five most impactful steps you can take to improve your performance on the test. We start at the beginning with study planning and move through the preparation process, all the way to the testing strategies that will help you get the most out of what you know when you're finally sitting in front of the test.

We recommend that you start preparing for your test as far in advance as possible. However, if you've bought this guide as a last-minute study resource and only have a few days before your test, we recommend that you skip over the first two Secret Keys since they address a long-term study plan.

If you struggle with **test anxiety**, we strongly encourage you to check out our recommendations for how you can overcome it. Test anxiety is a formidable foe, but it can be beaten, and we want to make sure you have the tools you need to defeat it.

Secret Key #1 – Plan Big, Study Small

There's a lot riding on your performance. If you want to ace this test, you're going to need to keep your skills sharp and the material fresh in your mind. You need a plan that lets you review everything you need to know while still fitting in your schedule. We'll break this strategy down into three categories.

Information Organization

Start with the information you already have: the official test outline. From this, you can make a complete list of all the concepts you need to cover before the test. Organize these concepts into groups that can be studied together, and create a list of any related vocabulary you need to learn so you can brush up on any difficult terms. You'll want to keep this vocabulary list handy once you actually start studying since you may need to add to it along the way.

Time Management

Once you have your set of study concepts, decide how to spread them out over the time you have left before the test. Break your study plan into small, clear goals so you have a manageable task for each day and know exactly what you're doing. Then just focus on one small step at a time. When you manage your time this way, you don't need to spend hours at a time studying. Studying a small block of content for a short period each day helps you retain information better and avoid stressing over how much you have left to do. You can relax knowing that you have a plan to cover everything in time. In order for this strategy to be effective though, you have to start studying early and stick to your schedule. Avoid the exhaustion and futility that comes from last-minute cramming!

Study Environment

The environment you study in has a big impact on your learning. Studying in a coffee shop, while probably more enjoyable, is not likely to be as fruitful as studying in a quiet room. It's important to keep distractions to a minimum. You're only planning to study for a short block of time, so make the most of it. Don't pause to check your phone or get up to find a snack. It's also important to **avoid multitasking**. Research has consistently shown that multitasking will make your studying dramatically less effective. Your study area should also be comfortable and well-lit so you don't have the distraction of straining your eyes or sitting on an uncomfortable chair.

The time of day you study is also important. You want to be rested and alert. Don't wait until just before bedtime. Study when you'll be most likely to comprehend and remember. Even better, if you know what time of day your test will be, set that time aside for study. That way your brain will be used to working on that subject at that specific time and you'll have a better chance of recalling information.

Finally, it can be helpful to team up with others who are studying for the same test. Your actual studying should be done in as isolated an environment as possible, but the work of organizing the information and setting up the study plan can be divided up. In between study sessions, you can discuss with your teammates the concepts that you're all studying and quiz each other on the details. Just be sure that your teammates are as serious about the test as you are. If you find that your study time is being replaced with social time, you might need to find a new team.

Secret Key #2 – Make Your Studying Count

You're devoting a lot of time and effort to preparing for this test, so you want to be absolutely certain it will pay off. This means doing more than just reading the content and hoping you can remember it on test day. It's important to make every minute of study count. There are two main areas you can focus on to make your studying count:

Retention

It doesn't matter how much time you study if you can't remember the material. You need to make sure you are retaining the concepts. To check your retention of the information you're learning, try recalling it at later times with minimal prompting. Try carrying around flashcards and glance at one or two from time to time or ask a friend who's also studying for the test to quiz you.

To enhance your retention, look for ways to put the information into practice so that you can apply it rather than simply recalling it. If you're using the information in practical ways, it will be much easier to remember. Similarly, it helps to solidify a concept in your mind if you're not only reading it to yourself but also explaining it to someone else. Ask a friend to let you teach them about a concept you're a little shaky on (or speak aloud to an imaginary audience if necessary). As you try to summarize, define, give examples, and answer your friend's questions, you'll understand the concepts better and they will stay with you longer. Finally, step back for a big picture view and ask yourself how each piece of information fits with the whole subject. When you link the different concepts together and see them working together as a whole, it's easier to remember the individual components.

Finally, practice showing your work on any multi-step problems, even if you're just studying. Writing out each step you take to solve a problem will help solidify the process in your mind, and you'll be more likely to remember it during the test.

Modality

Modality simply refers to the means or method by which you study. Choosing a study modality that fits your own individual learning style is crucial. No two people learn best in exactly the same way, so it's important to know your strengths and use them to your advantage.

For example, if you learn best by visualization, focus on visualizing a concept in your mind and draw an image or a diagram. Try color-coding your notes, illustrating them, or creating symbols that will trigger your mind to recall a learned concept. If you learn best by hearing or discussing information, find a study partner who learns the same way or read aloud to yourself. Think about how to put the information in your own words. Imagine that you are giving a lecture on the topic and record yourself so you can listen to it later.

For any learning style, flashcards can be helpful. Organize the information so you can take advantage of spare moments to review. Underline key words or phrases. Use different colors for different categories. Mnemonic devices (such as creating a short list in which every item starts with the same letter) can also help with retention. Find what works best for you and use it to store the information in your mind most effectively and easily.

Secret Key #3 – Practice the Right Way

Your success on test day depends not only on how many hours you put into preparing, but also on whether you prepared the right way. It's good to check along the way to see if your studying is paying off. One of the most effective ways to do this is by taking practice tests to evaluate your progress. Practice tests are useful because they show exactly where you need to improve. Every time you take a practice test, pay special attention to these three groups of questions:

- The questions you got wrong
- The questions you had to guess on, even if you guessed right
- The questions you found difficult or slow to work through

This will show you exactly what your weak areas are, and where you need to devote more study time. Ask yourself why each of these questions gave you trouble. Was it because you didn't understand the material? Was it because you didn't remember the vocabulary? Do you need more repetitions on this type of question to build speed and confidence? Dig into those questions and figure out how you can strengthen your weak areas as you go back to review the material.

Additionally, many practice tests have a section explaining the answer choices. It can be tempting to read the explanation and think that you now have a good understanding of the concept. However, an explanation likely only covers part of the question's broader context. Even if the explanation makes sense, **go back and investigate** every concept related to the question until you're positive you have a thorough understanding.

As you go along, keep in mind that the practice test is just that: practice. Memorizing these questions and answers will not be very helpful on the actual test because it is unlikely to have any of the same exact questions. If you only know the right answers to the sample questions, you won't be prepared for the real thing. **Study the concepts** until you understand them fully, and then you'll be able to answer any question that shows up on the test.

It's important to wait on the practice tests until you're ready. If you take a test on your first day of study, you may be overwhelmed by the amount of material covered and how much you need to learn. Work up to it gradually.

On test day, you'll need to be prepared for answering questions, managing your time, and using the test-taking strategies you've learned. It's a lot to balance, like a mental marathon that will have a big impact on your future. Like training for a marathon, you'll need to start slowly and work your way up. When test day arrives, you'll be ready.

Start with the strategies you've read in the first two Secret Keys—plan your course and study in the way that works best for you. If you have time, consider using multiple study resources to get different approaches to the same concepts. It can be helpful to see difficult concepts from more than one angle. Then find a good source for practice tests. Many times, the test website will suggest potential study resources or provide sample tests.

Practice Test Strategy

If you're able to find at least three practice tests, we recommend this strategy:

Untimed and Open-Book Practice

Take the first test with no time constraints and with your notes and study guide handy. Take your time and focus on applying the strategies you've learned.

Timed and Open-Book Practice

Take the second practice test open-book as well, but set a timer and practice pacing yourself to finish in time.

Timed and Closed-Book Practice

Take any other practice tests as if it were test day. Set a timer and put away your study materials. Sit at a table or desk in a quiet room, imagine yourself at the testing center, and answer questions as quickly and accurately as possible.

Keep repeating timed and closed-book tests on a regular basis until you run out of practice tests or it's time for the actual test. Your mind will be ready for the schedule and stress of test day, and you'll be able to focus on recalling the material you've learned.

Secret Key #4 – Pace Yourself

Once you're fully prepared for the material on the test, your biggest challenge on test day will be managing your time. Just knowing that the clock is ticking can make you panic even if you have plenty of time left. Work on pacing yourself so you can build confidence against the time constraints of the exam. Pacing is a difficult skill to master, especially in a high-pressure environment, so **practice is vital**.

Set time expectations for your pace based on how much time is available. For example, if a section has 60 questions and the time limit is 30 minutes, you know you have to average 30 seconds or less per question in order to answer them all. Although 30 seconds is the hard limit, set 25 seconds per question as your goal, so you reserve extra time to spend on harder questions. When you budget extra time for the harder questions, you no longer have any reason to stress when those questions take longer to answer.

Don't let this time expectation distract you from working through the test at a calm, steady pace, but keep it in mind so you don't spend too much time on any one question. Recognize that taking extra time on one question you don't understand may keep you from answering two that you do understand later in the test. If your time limit for a question is up and you're still not sure of the answer, mark it and move on, and come back to it later if the time and the test format allow. If the testing format doesn't allow you to return to earlier questions, just make an educated guess; then put it out of your mind and move on.

On the easier questions, be careful not to rush. It may seem wise to hurry through them so you have more time for the challenging ones, but it's not worth missing one if you know the concept and just didn't take the time to read the question fully. Work efficiently but make sure you understand the question and have looked at all of the answer choices, since more than one may seem right at first.

Even if you're paying attention to the time, you may find yourself a little behind at some point. You should speed up to get back on track, but do so wisely. Don't panic; just take a few seconds less on each question until you're caught up. Don't guess without thinking, but do look through the answer choices and eliminate any you know are wrong. If you can get down to two choices, it is often worthwhile to guess from those. Once you've chosen an answer, move on and don't dwell on any that you skipped or had to hurry through. If a question was taking too long, chances are it was one of the harder ones, so you weren't as likely to get it right anyway.

On the other hand, if you find yourself getting ahead of schedule, it may be beneficial to slow down a little. The more quickly you work, the more likely you are to make a careless mistake that will affect your score. You've budgeted time for each question, so don't be afraid to spend that time. Practice an efficient but careful pace to get the most out of the time you have.

Secret Key #5 – Have a Plan for Guessing

When you're taking the test, you may find yourself stuck on a question. Some of the answer choices seem better than others, but you don't see the one answer choice that is obviously correct. What do you do?

The scenario described above is very common, yet most test takers have not effectively prepared for it. Developing and practicing a plan for guessing may be one of the single most effective uses of your time as you get ready for the exam.

In developing your plan for guessing, there are three questions to address:

- When should you start the guessing process?
- How should you narrow down the choices?
- Which answer should you choose?

When to Start the Guessing Process

Unless your plan for guessing is to select C every time (which, despite its merits, is not what we recommend), you need to leave yourself enough time to apply your answer elimination strategies. Since you have a limited amount of time for each question, that means that if you're going to give yourself the best shot at guessing correctly, you have to decide quickly whether or not you will guess.

Of course, the best-case scenario is that you don't have to guess at all, so first, see if you can answer the question based on your knowledge of the subject and basic reasoning skills. Focus on the key words in the question and try to jog your memory of related topics. Give yourself a chance to bring the knowledge to mind, but once you realize that you don't have (or you can't access) the knowledge you need to answer the question, it's time to start the guessing process.

It's almost always better to start the guessing process too early than too late. It only takes a few seconds to remember something and answer the question from knowledge. Carefully eliminating wrong answer choices takes longer. Plus, going through the process of eliminating answer choices can actually help jog your memory.

Summary: Start the guessing process as soon as you decide that you can't answer the question based on your knowledge.

How to Narrow Down the Choices

The next chapter in this book (**Test-Taking Strategies**) includes a wide range of strategies for how to approach questions and how to look for answer choices to eliminate. You will definitely want to read those carefully, practice them, and figure out which ones work best for you. Here though, we're going to address a mindset rather than a particular strategy.

Your chances of guessing an answer correctly depend on how many options you are choosing from.

How many choices you have	How likely you are to guess correctly
5	20%
4	25%
3	33%
2	50%
1	100%

You can see from this chart just how valuable it is to be able to eliminate incorrect answers and make an educated guess, but there are two things that many test takers do that cause them to miss out on the benefits of guessing:

- Accidentally eliminating the correct answer
- Selecting an answer based on an impression

We'll look at the first one here, and the second one in the next section.

To avoid accidentally eliminating the correct answer, we recommend a thought exercise called **the $5 challenge**. In this challenge, you only eliminate an answer choice from contention if you are willing to bet $5 on it being wrong. Why $5? Five dollars is a small but not insignificant amount of money. It's an amount you could afford to lose but wouldn't want to throw away. And while losing $5 once might not hurt too much, doing it twenty times will set you back $100. In the same way, each small decision you make—eliminating a choice here, guessing on a question there—won't by itself impact your score very much, but when you put them all together, they can make a big difference. By holding each answer choice elimination decision to a higher standard, you can reduce the risk of accidentally eliminating the correct answer.

The $5 challenge can also be applied in a positive sense: If you are willing to bet $5 that an answer choice *is* correct, go ahead and mark it as correct.

Summary: Only eliminate an answer choice if you are willing to bet $5 that it is wrong.

Which Answer to Choose

You're taking the test. You've run into a hard question and decided you'll have to guess. You've eliminated all the answer choices you're willing to bet $5 on. Now you have to pick an answer. Why do we even need to talk about this? Why can't you just pick whichever one you feel like when the time comes?

The answer to these questions is that if you don't come into the test with a plan, you'll rely on your impression to select an answer choice, and if you do that, you risk falling into a trap. The test writers know that everyone who takes their test will be guessing on some of the questions, so they intentionally write wrong answer choices to seem plausible. You still have to pick an answer though, and if the wrong answer choices are designed to look right, how can you ever be sure that you're not falling for their trap? The best solution we've found to this dilemma is to take the decision out of your hands entirely. Here is the process we recommend:

Once you've eliminated any choices that you are confident (willing to bet $5) are wrong, select the first remaining choice as your answer.

Whether you choose to select the first remaining choice, the second, or the last, the important thing is that you use some preselected standard. Using this approach guarantees that you will not be enticed into selecting an answer choice that looks right, because you are not basing your decision on how the answer choices look.

This is not meant to make you question your knowledge. Instead, it is to help you recognize the difference between your knowledge and your impressions. There's a huge difference between thinking an answer is right because of what you know, and thinking an answer is right because it looks or sounds like it should be right.

Summary: To ensure that your selection is appropriately random, make a predetermined selection from among all answer choices you have not eliminated.

Test-Taking Strategies

This section contains a list of test-taking strategies that you may find helpful as you work through the test. By taking what you know and applying logical thought, you can maximize your chances of answering any question correctly!

It is very important to realize that every question is different and every person is different: no single strategy will work on every question, and no single strategy will work for every person. That's why we've included all of them here, so you can try them out and determine which ones work best for different types of questions and which ones work best for you.

Question Strategies

Read Carefully

Read the question and answer choices carefully. Don't miss the question because you misread the terms. You have plenty of time to read each question thoroughly and make sure you understand what is being asked. Yet a happy medium must be attained, so don't waste too much time. You must read carefully, but efficiently.

Contextual Clues

Look for contextual clues. If the question includes a word you are not familiar with, look at the immediate context for some indication of what the word might mean. Contextual clues can often give you all the information you need to decipher the meaning of an unfamiliar word. Even if you can't determine the meaning, you may be able to narrow down the possibilities enough to make a solid guess at the answer to the question.

Prefixes

If you're having trouble with a word in the question or answer choices, try dissecting it. Take advantage of every clue that the word might include. Prefixes and suffixes can be a huge help. Usually they allow you to determine a basic meaning. Pre- means before, post- means after, pro - is positive, de- is negative. From prefixes and suffixes, you can get an idea of the general meaning of the word and try to put it into context.

Hedge Words

Watch out for critical hedge words, such as *likely, may, can, sometimes, often, almost, mostly, usually, generally, rarely,* and *sometimes.* Question writers insert these hedge phrases to cover every possibility. Often an answer choice will be wrong simply because it leaves no room for exception. Be on guard for answer choices that have definitive words such as *exactly* and *always.*

Switchback Words

Stay alert for *switchbacks.* These are the words and phrases frequently used to alert you to shifts in thought. The most common switchback words are *but, although,* and *however.* Others include *nevertheless, on the other hand, even though, while, in spite of, despite, regardless of.* Switchback words are important to catch because they can change the direction of the question or an answer choice.

Face Value

When in doubt, use common sense. Accept the situation in the problem at face value. Don't read too much into it. These problems will not require you to make wild assumptions. If you have to go beyond creativity and warp time or space in order to have an answer choice fit the question, then you should move on and consider the other answer choices. These are normal problems rooted in reality. The applicable relationship or explanation may not be readily apparent, but it is there for you to figure out. Use your common sense to interpret anything that isn't clear.

Answer Choice Strategies

Answer Selection

The most thorough way to pick an answer choice is to identify and eliminate wrong answers until only one is left, then confirm it is the correct answer. Sometimes an answer choice may immediately seem right, but be careful. The test writers will usually put more than one reasonable answer choice on each question, so take a second to read all of them and make sure that the other choices are not equally obvious. As long as you have time left, it is better to read every answer choice than to pick the first one that looks right without checking the others.

Answer Choice Families

An answer choice family consists of two (in rare cases, three) answer choices that are very similar in construction and cannot all be true at the same time. If you see two answer choices that are direct opposites or parallels, one of them is usually the correct answer. For instance, if one answer choice says that quantity x increases and another either says that quantity x decreases (opposite) or says that quantity y increases (parallel), then those answer choices would fall into the same family. An answer choice that doesn't match the construction of the answer choice family is more likely to be incorrect. Most questions will not have answer choice families, but when they do appear, you should be prepared to recognize them.

Eliminate Answers

Eliminate answer choices as soon as you realize they are wrong, but make sure you consider all possibilities. If you are eliminating answer choices and realize that the last one you are left with is also wrong, don't panic. Start over and consider each choice again. There may be something you missed the first time that you will realize on the second pass.

Avoid Fact Traps

Don't be distracted by an answer choice that is factually true but doesn't answer the question. You are looking for the choice that answers the question. Stay focused on what the question is asking for so you don't accidentally pick an answer that is true but incorrect. Always go back to the question and make sure the answer choice you've selected actually answers the question and is not merely a true statement.

Extreme Statements

In general, you should avoid answers that put forth extreme actions as standard practice or proclaim controversial ideas as established fact. An answer choice that states the "process should be used in certain situations, if..." is much more likely to be correct than one that states the "process should be discontinued completely." The first is a calm rational statement and doesn't even make a definitive, uncompromising stance, using a hedge word *if* to provide wiggle room, whereas the second choice is a radical idea and far more extreme.

Benchmark

As you read through the answer choices and you come across one that seems to answer the question well, mentally select that answer choice. This is not your final answer, but it's the one that will help you evaluate the other answer choices. The one that you selected is your benchmark or standard for judging each of the other answer choices. Every other answer choice must be compared to your benchmark. That choice is correct until proven otherwise by another answer choice beating it. If you find a better answer, then that one becomes your new benchmark. Once you've decided that no other choice answers the question as well as your benchmark, you have your final answer.

Predict the Answer

Before you even start looking at the answer choices, it is often best to try to predict the answer. When you come up with the answer on your own, it is easier to avoid distractions and traps because you will know exactly what to look for. The right answer choice is unlikely to be word-for-word what you came up with, but it should be a close match. Even if you are confident that you have the right answer, you should still take the time to read each option before moving on.

General Strategies

Tough Questions

If you are stumped on a problem or it appears too hard or too difficult, don't waste time. Move on! Remember though, if you can quickly check for obviously incorrect answer choices, your chances of guessing correctly are greatly improved. Before you completely give up, at least try to knock out a couple of possible answers. Eliminate what you can and then guess at the remaining answer choices before moving on.

Check Your Work

Since you will probably not know every term listed and the answer to every question, it is important that you get credit for the ones that you do know. Don't miss any questions through careless mistakes. If at all possible, try to take a second to look back over your answer selection and make sure you've selected the correct answer choice and haven't made a costly careless mistake (such as marking an answer choice that you didn't mean to mark). This quick double check should more than pay for itself in caught mistakes for the time it costs.

Pace Yourself

It's easy to be overwhelmed when you're looking at a page full of questions; your mind is confused and full of random thoughts, and the clock is ticking down faster than you would like. Calm down and maintain the pace that you have set for yourself. Especially as you get down to the last few minutes of the test, don't let the small numbers on the clock make you panic. As long as you are on track by monitoring your pace, you are guaranteed to have time for each question.

Don't Rush

It is very easy to make errors when you are in a hurry. Maintaining a fast pace in answering questions is pointless if it makes you miss questions that you would have gotten right otherwise. Test writers like to include distracting information and wrong answers that seem right. Taking a little extra time to avoid careless mistakes can make all the difference in your test score. Find a pace that allows you to be confident in the answers that you select.

Keep Moving

Panicking will not help you pass the test, so do your best to stay calm and keep moving. Taking deep breaths and going through the answer elimination steps you practiced can help to break through a stress barrier and keep your pace.

Final Notes

The combination of a solid foundation of content knowledge and the confidence that comes from practicing your plan for applying that knowledge is the key to maximizing your performance on test day. As your foundation of content knowledge is built up and strengthened, you'll find that the strategies included in this chapter become more and more effective in helping you quickly sift through the distractions and traps of the test to isolate the correct answer.

Now it's time to move on to the test content chapters of this book, but be sure to keep your goal in mind. As you read, think about how you will be able to apply this information on the test. If you've already seen sample questions for the test and you have an idea of the question format and style, try to come up with questions of your own that you can answer based on what you're reading. This will give you valuable practice applying your knowledge in the same ways you can expect to on test day.

Good luck and good studying!

Reading Assessment

Determining word meaning

A reader may encounter an unfamiliar word on the STAAR test but can figure out the meaning of the word based on their previous knowledge of word usage in different situations. Words may be used to describe an action, a location, or what something looks like, how it feels, smells, tastes, or sounds. Readers can use their own experience with situations and the format of a sentence to decide what the author is trying to tell them. For example, a reader may know that use of the preposition *on* refers to the location of an object. Look at the use of *on* in the following sentence:

> A vase of flowers was placed on the bureau in the bedroom.

If the reader did not know what bureau meant, he or she could decide from experience with the preposition *on* that a bureau is low enough to reach and place a vase on top of. The reader may then decide, based on experience, that a bureau is a piece of furniture found in a bedroom.

On the STAAR test, words will be used that the test taker is often unfamiliar with. To find the meaning of an unfamiliar word, a test taker needs to look at the context of the word. Context means the words and sentences surrounding the unfamiliar word. Look at how a word is used in a sentence. Also, look at the root words used in a sentence. For example, suppose the STAAR test contains the following sentence: Viewers were *disinterested* in the display of modern art at the local museum. If the reader did not know what *disinterested* meant, he or she could look at the rest of the sentence. The reader knows that the sentence is about viewing art. In addition, the reader knows that the prefix *dis-* means not. The reader can therefore decide that the display at the museum was not enjoyed by viewers.

Multiple-meaning words

A multiple-meaning word has different definitions in the dictionary. Many words have multiple meanings, so the reader has to pay attention to how a word is used in a sentence to figure out which meaning is intended. A multiple-meaning word is spelled the same, no matter how it is used. So to find the meaning of a multiple-meaning word, the reader needs to look at the information presented in the rest of the sentence. For example, look at the word *leaves* in the following two sentences:

- Michelle *leaves* the building at 5 o'clock every day.
- The *leaves* fell off the oak tree in September.

In the first sentence, *leaves* means exits. In the second sentence, *leaves* refers to parts of a tree. By looking at the rest of each sentence, the reader can understand which definition of the multiple-meaning word the author is referring to.

Root words, prefixes, and suffixes

A root word is the main part of a word, without any prefixes or suffixes added onto it. A root word is the original form of the word. For example, the root word pay means to give something, such as money, in exchange for something else. When a prefix or suffix is added on to the root, or main word, the meaning of the word can change. For example, the word prepay means to give money before a good or service is provided. A person may prepay for a class. The word repay, with the prefix re-, means to give money back. A prefix or suffix can change the meaning of the whole word.

A prefix is found before a root, or main part, of a word. For example, in the word unhappy, the prefix is un-, which means not. A suffix is found at the end of a root word. For example, in the word unhappiest, the suffix is -est, which means most or greatest. By looking at prefixes and suffixes, which are also called affixes, the reader can figure out what is meant by a word.

Student lists of prefixes and suffixes will vary. A few examples of prefixes include un-, pre-, and dis-. The prefixes mean not, before, and not, respectively. A few examples of suffixes include -ing, -er, and -est. The suffixes mean right now, greater than, and greatest respectively. An affix is anything that is added to a root word to show degree, variety, or establish meaning.

A reader can use root words and prefixes to figure out the general meaning of an unknown word. In the word *dislike*, the prefix dis- means not, lack of, or away from. The root word *like* means to enjoy. With the prefix dis- added on to *like*, the full word *dislike* means to not enjoy.

By adding the prefix dis- to a word, the word attains its opposite meaning. Some other words containing the prefix dis- that add the opposite meaning to a word include discover, disable, and disjointed. By adding an affix, whether a prefix or suffix, to a word, the meaning of the word in its entirety is altered.

Example 1

Based on experience, determine the meaning of *paddled* in the following sentence:

> The canoers *paddled* down the swiftly moving river toward the shore.

In the example, *paddled* refers to the action that the canoers are taking in the sentence. A canoe is a type of boat, which the reader may know based on experience. The canoers are moving the boat toward the side of the river. The reader may also know that canoers need to use their arms to move a boat, an action called *paddling*. The reader may know, too, that swiftly means to move quickly. If a river is moving swiftly, then the canoers may want to head toward the side of the river, which would require them to take the action called *paddling*. By combining their own experience with clues in the wording of a sentence, the reader can often figure out the meaning of an unfamiliar word.

Example 2

Using context clues, determine the meaning of the word *breeches* in the following sentence:

> "He was wearing the blue canvas *breeches* when he walked out on the shingle" (from "How the Whale Got His Throat" by Rudyard Kipling).

Context clues are words in the sentence and surrounding sentences that help the reader to figure out the meaning of a new word. In this example, *breeches* refers to what the character was wearing. The reader knows that the character was walking while wearing the breeches and that they were made of blue canvas. The reader can therefore conclude that breeches are a pair of pants worn by the character. By using the information around a word in a sentence, the overall meaning of a word in context can be understood. Using context clues to figure out meaning can be helpful when learning a new set of vocabulary words or reading a difficult text. The dictionary definition of a word can always be looked up to verify intended meaning.

<u>Example 3</u>

Read the following sentence and determine the meaning of the word *spellbound* based on context clues:

> "Little Charlie Bucket was staring at her absolutely *spellbound*, watching her huge rubbery lips as they pressed and unpressed with the chewing, and Grandpa Joe stood beside him, gaping at the girl" (from *Charlie and the Chocolate Factory*, by Roald Dahl).

Context clues are key words within a sentence that help the reader to find meaning for a new word. In the context of the sentence, *spellbound* refers to not being able to turn away. The character Little Charlie Bucket is staring at a girl as she chews, which means that he is looking at her without moving. The character Grandpa Joe is looking at the girl as well, while standing right next to Charlie. The reader can decide, based on the sentence, that the two characters are viewing something unusual and do not want to look away. Even if the reader does not know the meaning of an unfamiliar word, looking at the surrounding sentence or sentences can help the reader to figure out the meaning.

<u>Example 4</u>

Using current knowledge of prefixes and suffixes, determine the meaning of the word *unluckiest* in the following sentence:

> He felt like the *unluckiest* person in the neighborhood when his garden did not grow.

A reader may know that *lucky* means good things tend to happen to a person. Using knowledge of prefixes and suffixes, the meaning of the word *unluckiest* as a whole can be figured out. The prefix un- means not and the suffix -est means most. Putting the entire word together, the reader can see that *unluckiest* means that a person has the most bad luck. This makes sense in the context of the sentence. If a person's garden did not grow, they would be upset and feel like good things did not happen to them. If the prefix un- was removed from the word, *luckiest* would refer to a person who has good things happen to them the most. By paying close attention to the meaning of a root word plus any prefixes and suffixes, the reader can figure out what the author is trying to say.

Using dictionaries and glossaries

A dictionary is a separate reference book with definitions of words in the English language as well as pronunciation and etymological information. A glossary is a list of terms and their definitions that can be found at the back of some types of books, like textbooks and reference books. Dictionaries and glossaries both give definitions of words. A glossary does not have definitions of all words, like a dictionary, but rather a glossary gives only definitions for the important terms in the book, which are either uncommon or newly introduced. A glossary may be used when reading a book about economics, for example, to help define technical terms, or it may be used when reading a chapter in a science textbook.

Fiction

Fiction is a general term for any form of literary narrative that is invented or imagined rather than factual. For those individuals who equate fact with truth, the imagined or invented character of fiction tends to render it relatively unimportant or trivial among the genres. Defenders of fiction are quick to point out that the fictional mode is an essential part of being. The ability to imagine or discuss what-if plots, characters, and events is clearly part of the human experience.

Fiction is much wider than simply prose fiction. Songs, ballads, epics, and narrative poems are also examples of fiction. A full definition of fiction must include not only the work itself but also the framework in which it is read. Literary fiction can also be defined as not true rather than nonexistent, as many works of historical fiction refer to real people, places, and events that are treated imaginatively as if they were true. These imaginary elements enrich and broaden literary expression.

Nonfiction

Nonfiction is a story based on real facts and information. Examples include biographies and autobiographies.

<u>Biography</u>

A biography is a detailed account written about a specific person's life and their experiences. Biographies include what a person did throughout their lifetime and how those actions influenced their world and the world around them. A biography tells about the person's personality and character, whether it be good or bad. The author of a biography often studies diary entries and other personal letters to get as much valid information about the person they are writing about.

<u>Autobiography</u>

An autobiography is an account of a person's life also, but is written by the person. Autobiographies are often written because the author has experienced something bad or good that they want to tell the world about. Other times autobiographies are written to tell about a person's life from childhood to adulthood and their experiences along the way. Autobiographies can often be a mix of factual and fictional information. The author can skew the story to have a positive ending.

Purpose

An author may write a story to:

- Inform
- Persuade/Influence
- Express
- Entertain

The author may inform the reader about a topic so that the reader learns something new. For example, an informative paper on kangaroos would detail where kangaroos live, what they look like, what they eat, and other habits.

An author may wish to persuade or influence the reader on a given topic. The author typically has a point of view on the topic. For example, an author may try to persuade the reader that the library is the best place to go in the summer when it is hot outside. The author would present information about the library and explain *why* it is a good place to visit. An author may also wish to simply express a point of view. For example, the author may think that a new park in town is a good idea, and write an essay about why the park is excellent for the community.

Sometimes a story is simply meant to entertain the reader. Fictional stories are often meant to amuse the reader with a series of interesting events.

<u>Example</u>

Read the following sentence. State the author's point in writing the sentence, whether it is to inform, entertain, persuade, or state an opinion:

The rollercoaster reached a peak and paused for a second, before gliding down the other side of the hill with a roar.

The purpose of the sentence is to entertain the reader. The author does not state his or her opinion on the topic, nor is the sentence meant to inform the reader about an important topic. The sentence does not persuade the reader to accept a certain point of view. Text in fictional pieces such as short stories and novels is often meant to entertain the reader.

Note that the text describes an event, rather than an issue or conflict. The event is part of a larger tale, where a series of events occur to form an entire story. The reader may notice that the author uses descriptive words to present the setting, such as gliding and roar. The reader can better picture a story when the setting is clearly presented.

Summary

A summary states the main points of a story. Every summary should include the following:

- The main idea of the story
- Key points of the story
- The conclusion of the story
- Important information that the author wants the reader to take from the story

A summary is typically one paragraph in length. Only important information, rather than supporting paragraphs and details, is included in a summary. For a long story with multiple settings and scenes, a summary may be a few paragraphs in length. These paragraphs give the main points of each major part of the story. The summary of a long story always includes a conclusion to wrap up the story as an entirety.

Structural elements of poetry

Meter is the rhythm pattern of a verse or part of a verse in poetry. Rhyme is when you have identical or very similar sounds on the ends or in the middle of lines in a poem. These patterns in the lines of poetry are called feet. Line breaks are how the poem is divided up. Stanzas are composed of a certain number of lines that help with the flow of the poem.

Different types of poetry have different structures. Some use only meter to create structure. Lyrical poetry was originally accompanied with a lyre and does not necessarily have to rhyme. It uses meters to set the structure and flow of the poem. Some types of poetry do not follow a structure. Free verse does not use rhyme or meter consistently in the poem. Often the author uses lines to give the poem some sort of rhythm. Free verse poems can be very different from one another.

Structural elements of dramatic literature

Dramatic literature follows a pattern. First is the introduction, where you find out the characters, the setting, and the conflict that exists in the story. The next element is called rising action. This is the smaller conflicts the main character will struggle with that also occur within the text. The climax is where a change occurs, which can be good or bad for the main character. Falling action is where the main character is aware of the conflict in the story and either overcomes the problem or has to deal with a negative outcome. The resolution is the conclusion of the story. This includes everything that occurs between the falling action and the final scene.

Character relationships and changes

Each story will have many different types of characters and each of these characters will have a different relationship with other characters. Stories usually have a protagonist, antagonist, and a variety of other characters including round, flat, and stock characters. The protagonist and antagonist oppose each other, so their relationship is almost always one of dislike. A flat character is one that does not have any substantial changes throughout the story. Round characters, by contrast, are major characters in the story and they will be more fully developed. They will usually encounter some type of conflict that they must overcome. Stock characters will often get their characteristics and mannerisms from widely known cultural stereotypes.

Plot, setting, and problem resolution

The plot of a story is a sequence of events that create the story. A plot is a series of events with a starting point, actions that occur, and a conclusion. Including a plot is important to form an entire story. Without a plot, nothing happens.

A story must start out with a *setting*. Sometimes a setting is obvious, and sometimes the reader must imagine where the story is taking place. A setting must be believable according to the plot of the story. The more detail an author gives about a setting, the better a reader is able to picture and understand where the story is occurring.

Every story must conclude in some way. *Problem resolution* often occurs at the end of a story, after a sequence of events has been carried out. Characters may find a solution to a problem with another character or a particular situation. Problem resolution wraps up the story for the reader.

<u>Plot sequence</u>

Read the following plot and analyze what the missing event is in the plot sequence:

> Jamika read the story that was assigned for homework. She placed her book in her backpack near the front door when she was finished. The teacher asked students to take out their books in class. Jamika did not have her book or backpack.

The reader has to guess, based on the plot sequence, what happened between events. The character, Jamika, placed her book in her backpack near the front door before going to school. This action indicates that Jamika meant to take the book back to school for class. The reader can assume that Jamika forgot her backpack near the front door, since Jamika did not have those items in class. A number of other events could have happened, but based on the current plot sequence, it is likely that Jamika left her backpack near the front door.

By looking carefully at a series of events in a story, a reader can determine what is missing. Look for a jump in thought and events that indicate a missing action in the story. Based on the wording, or context, of the story, the reader can figure out what most likely happened between events in the plot of the story.

<u>Setting</u>

A setting is where the action in a story takes place. The setting can be on land, sea, or in the air. Setting also includes the time period when a story occurred. A story can take place in a short period of time or over many years. The setting of a story is what makes each story unique; the setting sets up the sequence of events in the story.

<u>Example</u>

Read the sentence below and state the setting of the story:

> "Every afternoon, as they were coming from school, the children used to go and play in the Giant's garden" (from *The Selfish Giant* by Oscar Wilde).

The story takes place in the Giant's garden. The reader does not know any further details about the garden at this point, except that the children played in the Giant's garden on the way home from school. The reader does know that something may have stopped the children from playing in the garden, because the words "used to" are included in the sentence. If the story is being told in the future, the author may be looking back at a time in the past when the characters were children. The reader can assume that the garden was an enjoyable place, since the children went there every afternoon.

Use of metaphors and similes to create imagery

A metaphor is a type of figurative language in which the writer equates one thing with a different thing. For instance, in the sentence "The bird was an arrow arcing through the sky," the arrow is serving as a metaphor for the bird. The point of a metaphor is to encourage the reader to think about the thing being described in a different way. Using this example, we are being asked to envision the bird's flight as being similar to the arc of an arrow, so we will imagine it to be swift, bending, etc. Metaphors are a way for the author to describe without being direct and obvious. Metaphors are a more lyrical and suggestive way of providing information. Note that the thing to which a metaphor refers will not always be mentioned explicitly by the author. For instance, consider the following description of a forest in winter: "Swaying skeletons reached for the sky and groaned as the wind blew through them." The author is clearly using skeletons as a metaphor for leafless trees. This metaphor creates a spooky tone while inspiring the reader's imagination.

A simile is a figurative expression similar to a metaphor, though it requires the use of a distancing word such as *like* or *as*. Some examples are "The sun was like an orange," "eager as a beaver," and "nimble as a mountain goat." Because a simile includes like or as, it creates a little space between the description and the thing being described. If an author says that a house was "like a shoebox," the tone is slightly different than if the author said that the house was a shoebox. In a simile, the author indicates an awareness that the description is not the same thing as the thing being described. In a metaphor, there is no such distinction, even though one may safely assume that the author is aware of it. This is a subtle difference, but authors will alternately use metaphors and similes depending on their intended tone.

Inference

An inference is a conclusion or generalization that the reader makes based on the information provided within a text. Certain facts are included to help a reader come to a specific conclusion. For example, a story may open with a man trudging through the snow on a cold winter day, dragging a sled behind him. The reader can logically infer from the setting of the story that the man is wearing heavy winter clothes in order to stay warm. Information is implied based on the setting of a story, which is why setting is an important element of the text. If the same man in the example was trudging down a beach on a hot summer day, dragging a surf board behind him, the reader would assume that the man is not wearing heavy clothes. The reader makes inferences based on their own experiences and the information presented to them in the story.

Text evidence

The term text evidence refers to information included in a text that supports the main point of the paper, from which a reader can draw conclusions or generalizations. The author will deliberately include key points that serve as supporting details for the main point of a paper. For example, the main point of a paper may state: The average yearly rainfall in the city has risen by 2 inches per year since 1999. The paper would go on to include the amount of rainfall for each month or season and any contributing factors that may be causing an increase in yearly rainfall. Additional facts, or text evidence to support the point that yearly rainfall is rising in the city would help to prove that the author's main point is correct.

Organization of a text

Authors have to organize information logically so the reader can follow it and locate information within the text. Two common organizational structures are cause and effect and chronological order. In cause and effect, an author presents one thing that makes something else happen. For example, if one were to go to bed very late, they would be tired. The cause is going to bed late, with the effect of being tired the next day. When using chronological order, the author presents information in the order that it happened. For example, biographies are written in chronological order; the subject's birth and childhood are presented first, followed by their adult life, and lastly by the events leading up to the person's death.

Motivation and conflict

The characters in a story all have past experiences that contribute to how they feel about a current situation. In real life, people have experiences that shape the way they think and feel. For example, a person may have baked cookies as a child, and associate the smell of cookies baking as an adult with their childhood kitchen. A person may feel like baking cookies when they want to feel comforted. Characters in a story act in the same way. They have what is called *motivation* based on things that have happened to them in the past. A character may feel scared of the ocean if they had a bad experience with swimming in the ocean. The character is then *motivated* to stay out of the ocean.

A *conflict* is a problem that needs to be solved. Conflicts can occur between characters in a story, or between a character and an object that does not move, such as a car that is in the way. The character or characters in a story need to solve a problem, or *conflict*, in order to move on in the story.

<u>Example 1</u>
Read the sentences below and state what the main conflict is at this point in the story:

> "They wandered about the whole night, and the next day, from morning till evening, but they could not find a path out of the wood. They were very hungry, too, for they had nothing to eat but a few berries they found growing on the ground" (from *Hansel and Gretel* by Hans Christian Andersen).

The characters in the story are lost in the woods. Although the characters are hungry, being hungry is a secondary conflict to the fact that they are lost. In order to resolve the conflict at this point in the story, the characters need to either find a way out of the woods themselves, or an alternative event will occur. The progression of events in the story is called the *plot*. When a conflict in a story is resolved, it is called *resolution*.

Based on the wording, or context, of the sentence, the reader can conclude that the characters do not enjoy being lost. The sentence indicates that the characters were wandering and hungry, words that are typically associated with not feeling happy. The reader can expect the characters to find a way out of the woods or for something else to happen to them, to continue the series of events, or *plot*, of the story.

Example 2

Read the following sentence and analyze the conflict between the two characters:

> Amy wanted to go to the park to play on the swings, while Hannah wanted to play house indoors.

The two characters have differing points of view. Amy wants to do one activity, while Hannah wants to do something entirely different. In order to resolve the conflict, the girls need to agree upon where they will spend their time. One person may have to give in and agree to do one activity now, and enjoy the activity that she really wants to do at a later time. If the characters have a limited amount of time, they will only be able to do one activity.

The conflict in the sentence is based on a situation, that is, the girls are deciding what to do. The main point of a story is to resolve conflict, although conflict is not always fully resolved by the end of a story. Characters in a story may find an agreeable solution, such as the two girls above agreeing on a different activity, or they may be stuck in a conflict and the plot (sequence of events) in the story will not progress.

Character traits

A list of character traits can include:

- Anything a character thinks
- Feelings
- How they look
- How they act

Examples of character traits include: angry, happy, sad, bored, quiet, loud, talkative, active, slow, blond, dark-skinned, tall, short, plump, skinny, clumsy, neat, smart, reads a lot, athletic, creative, wears glasses, wears shorts every day, and so on.

It is important to realize that a character trait is a way to describe a person in a story. Every character will be different, just as every person is different. When describing a character, an author needs to be thorough, so that the reader can picture what the character would likely do next. A character trait may be part of a person's personality, or it may be a characteristic they were born with. An example of a characteristic a person is born with is eye color.

Example

Read the following sentence. State a character trait found in the sentence:

> Jerod reacted angrily to the news that he would not be able to go camping over the weekend.

A character trait is a way that a person behaves, what they look like, or what they like/dislike. In the example sentence, the reader knows that the character, Jerod, enjoys camping. Jerod's reaction to the fact that he would not be able to go camping shows that he feels disappointed. He had been looking forward to the trip. The reader also knows that Jerod shows his emotions, he does not keep them a secret. Jerod is not likely to be shy about expressing his opinion.

All characters in a story have their own set of unique traits. By showing how characters are different, an author can tell the reader how a character is likely to respond in a given situation. Characters may have opposite traits, or some degree of similarity.

Points of view

Points of view include:

- First person
- Second person
- Third person

A first person point of view is used when a story is told through the eyes of a character. The author may use the words I and my to show what the character is thinking. Second person point of view tells a story using the pronoun you. This is the least common point of view. Third person point of view is used to tell a story about a character or group of characters from an outside viewpoint. For example, the author may use the words her, his, they, or a name to talk about a character or characters. The reader does not know what the character is thinking at all times when third person point of view is used. Third person point of view is a common way to show action in a story. It also allows the author to easily and realistically tell a story from more than one person's viewpoint.

Comparison of viewpoints

Read the following two viewpoints. Compare and contrast how the two viewpoints are similar and different:

> The best way to understand the meaning of a new word is to look it up in the dictionary.

> The meaning of an unfamiliar word can be understood by looking at any prefixes, affixes, and the root word itself.

The first viewpoint takes the stance that a person needs to use another book, the dictionary, to find the meaning of a word. The second viewpoint states that a person can understand a word just by looking at the parts of a word. Both viewpoints explain ways to find the definition of an unfamiliar word, but each viewpoint presents a different way to find the definition. The second viewpoint assumes that the person can figure out a word on their own, using previous knowledge of parts of a word. Note that the first viewpoint uses the word "best," while the second viewpoint does not. Two differing viewpoints will often overlap in relation to the topic that they are discussing.

Comparison

An author will often compare traits, or parts, of two things that are not similar in all regards. The author will show how two things that are usually different are the same in one or more ways. An author may use like or as to describe a similarity between two objects, situations, or people. Read the following sentence:

> His mood was as bright as a sunny day.

In the sentence, the author is comparing two different things: how the character is feeling, and a sunny day. The reader can assume that the character is happy, since bright and sunny are often associated with happiness. Note that as is used to compare the character's mood and the type of weather.

An author may also directly state that one object or person is another. For example: "The thick lawn is a comforting blanket" compares grass and a comforting blanket. These are two objects that are not similar in all regards, but are compared in one way in the sentence. Comparison helps the reader to understand the likeness between two different words.

Main idea and supporting details

A main idea needs to be written as a full sentence in the first one to two paragraphs of a story. When the main idea is presented right away to the reader, the reader knows what the paper or story will be about. A main idea can then be supported by writing additional details or points that show that the main idea is true or provide more details on that topic.

Often, an author will write a main idea or conflict in a story, then explain and support that idea over many paragraphs or pages. A main idea needs to be written without the words "I think" if the information is meant to be presented to the reader as being factual.

Example 1

Read the following summary of a story and state the main idea:

> Jane was nervous about starting school in the fall. Her family had moved from Minnesota to Alaska over the summer, and she did not know anyone her age in the new town. One day in August a girl named Alicia said hi to her in the store, and they became friends.

The main idea in the summary is that Jane just moved and did not know anyone until she became friends with Alicia. A summary needs to focus on Jane moving and meeting her new friend, Alicia. The fact that Jane was nervous about starting school gives the reader an idea of how Jane was feeling, but it is not the main focus of the story. Supporting details for the main idea include where and when Jane moved, along with where Jane met Alicia. Jane moved from Minnesota to Alaska, her new location, with her family and met Alicia at the store in August. The reader can assume that Jane was not as nervous about starting school after she met her new friend, Alicia.

Example 2

Read the following two sentences. State which sentence is a main idea and which sentence is a supporting detail. Explain the difference between the two sentences:

> She went fishing with her cousin Vinny.

> Jayden visited her relatives in Louisiana over the summer.

The first sentence is a supporting detail, and the second sentence is the main idea. A main idea gives the overall concept, or point, of the story. A supporting detail adds more information to the point of the story. The reader already knows that the name of the character needs to be introduced before using the pronoun she. Therefore, it makes sense that Jayden visiting her relatives in Louisiana over the summer must come before the supporting detail about her going fishing with her cousin Vinny. Once the reader knows the overall point of the text, supporting details help to explain what else happens in the story. The reader knows from the main point that the character Jayden is visiting her relatives in Louisiana, which is where she went fishing.

<u>Example 3</u>

Read the following main idea of a story and write a supporting detail for it:

> Madison's favorite thing to talk about was strawberries.

A good supporting detail would need to include information that supports or explains more about the main idea. A supporting detail might read: "She also loved to eat them," or "She also grew strawberries in her backyard." Supporting details provide additional information about the main idea that has not already been presented to the reader. A supporting detail further develops the topic of the story and provides an explanation of a part of the main idea.

In the example supporting details above, note that the topic is still focused on the subject of strawberries and action that the character takes in relation to that particular subject. A main idea will often appear in the first one to two paragraphs of a story. Supporting details appear later in a paragraph or in other paragraphs within the story.

<u>Example 4</u>

Determine the main idea that the following sentence tells the reader. Indicate what details support the main idea:

> His legs ached with each step up the steep mountainside, but he could clearly see the top.

The main idea is what the author wants the reader to understand about the text. Details help to explain or support the main idea. A main idea usually states the point of an entire essay, article, or book, but a main idea can be simply stated in one sentence. The main idea in the sentence above is that the man or boy in the story is having a hard time climbing the mountain, but he is going to keep climbing to the top. Details to support this statement include the word ached, showing that the character's body hurts, steep, showing that the climb is difficult, and could clearly see the top, which indicates that the climber has hope of reaching the mountaintop.

<u>Example 5</u>

Decide whether the following sentence is the main point or a supporting point of a text and state where the information would be placed in an outline:

> Bobcats are fascinating animals that hunt their prey in the middle of the night.

The sentence is most likely the main point of a story. The story will branch off with additional details about what the bobcat looks like, what animals it hunts, where it lives, and other interesting facts about its habits. The main point of a story occurs in the first one to two paragraphs of text. When deciding whether a point is a main or supporting point, think about where it would be placed in a paper about the topic. In the example sentence, the reader knows that information has not previously been presented about when the bobcat hunts. Using the context of the sentence, the reader can assume that these fascinating animals are only beginning to be described.

<u>Main idea of paragraph vs. main idea of whole story</u>

To find the main idea in a paragraph, the reader needs to look for the topic sentence of the paragraph. The topic sentence is usually the first sentence in a paragraph. A topic sentence states what the rest of the paragraph is about and is supported by the rest of the sentences in the paragraph. For example, the main idea of a paragraph may state: Dolphins live in the Gulf of Mexico. The rest of the paragraph will give additional details about the dolphins in the Gulf of Mexico, such as the fact that they travel in groups.

The main idea for a whole story, however, may not be the first sentence in the story. However, the main idea is typically found within the first couple of paragraphs of the story. The main idea of a story is one sentence that tells what the rest of the story is about. Other paragraphs contain details that support the main idea.

Organization of information from stories

Information from a story can be organized into:

- An outline
- A timeline
- A graphic organizer

Organizing information from a text helps the reader to see what the main point is in a story, how supporting details are used, and how the story concludes. An outline, timeline, or graphic organizer allows the reader to look quickly at the main idea and supporting ideas in a story, without having to search for them through paragraphs of text. An outline will contain either capital letters or Roman numerals and lowercase letters or numbers for supporting points. A timeline presents ideas in the order in which they occurred over time. The beginning of a timeline is the beginning of a story. A graphic organizer, such as a spider-map, will present one main idea in a bubble or box, then have supporting ideas branching off the main idea. The main point of creating a form of organization is to easily recall where a point occurred in a story.

Drawing conclusions or generalizations

Each story has a main point and supporting points. The main point and supporting points of a story lead the reader to assume that a given point is true. Readers may come to their own conclusion about a topic, or the author may state a conclusion at the end of a story. When readers are in the middle of a story, they can predict what will happen at the end of it based on the events that have occurred so far and the typical characteristics that have been presented by the author up to that point. A reader needs to consider all of the information that an author has presented, including the main point and supporting points, to make a logical conclusion about the story.

Example 1
Read the following sentence. Draw a conclusion based upon the information presented:

> The hilltop was covered in low-lying clouds of grey, and a moist silence hung in the air as if the sky had drawn in a breath and paused.

The reader can conclude, or infer, based on the information in the sentence, that it is about to rain on the hilltop. The words used in the sentence give the reader clues to draw this conclusion. For example, the words low-lying clouds of grey indicate that rainclouds are present. A moist silence often occurs just before a storm. Based on the reader's own experience and the words presented in the sentence, the reader can conclude that the storm is about to break. Authors will often only present a certain amount of detail to the reader, and the reader needs to fill in the blanks. An author will give the reader just enough information to come to a logical conclusion without having to directly state that conclusion in the story.

<u>Example 2</u>

Draw a conclusion based on the following sentence from "The Sing-Song of Old Man Kangaroo" by Rudyard Kipling:

> "He hopped through the Flinders; he hopped through the Cinders; he hopped through the deserts in the middle of Australia."

Based on the wording in the sentence, the character appears to be a kangaroo. The fact that the character hopped through the deserts in the middle of Australia lends the reader to believe that the character is a kangaroo. The reader needs to use personal knowledge of geography, animals, and context clues to draw this conclusion. The title of the story includes the word kangaroo, as well, which gives the reader a clue that the character described in the story is that type of animal.

Using context clues, or wording in a sentence, is an important way to identify what the author is talking about in the story. An author will often leave blanks for the reader to fill in on their own, using information that has been presented up to that point in the story.

Fact and opinion

When an author presents a fact, the sentence is often supported with additional details. A fact does not use the words "I think" and is not based on what the author thinks about the topic. Information is presented as an absolute truth, with supporting details from expert sources included to show that the point is true.

An opinion will often include the words "I think" and is based on what the author thinks about a topic, not what has been proven to be true. An opinion often does not include expert sources and is not well accepted in a field of study. If an author presents information without providing evidence or points about why it is true, the information is most likely an opinion held by the author.

<u>Example</u>

Decide whether the following sentence is a fact or opinion. Explain your reasoning:

> Winter is the best season of the year, because the cold weather allows snow to fall in many states.

The example sentence is an opinion. The author believes that winter is the best season of the year, but that is the opinion of the author, not a fact. Part of the sentence is a fact: that cold weather allows snow to fall in many states. However, the sentence taken as a whole is an opinion. There is no best season; people just have their own preference and reasoning for which season they think is best. A fact about winter stated on its own may read: Cold temperatures over a long period of time make water freeze in the lakes of many states. This is a true statement about winter, not something that the author believes about the season based on his or her opinion.

Cause and effect and chronology

When an author uses *cause and effect* in a story, they present one idea and show how it leads to another. For example, an author may say: "It was hot outside, so Maddie did not go for a bike ride." The cause of Maddie not going for a bike ride is the heat. The effect is that Maddie decided not to go for a bike ride.

Chronology details the order that events occurred over time. This way of showing progression of ideas typically starts in the past or present, and works up to the present or future. For example, an author may say: "I woke up at 6 a.m. and went downstairs. I then ate breakfast, washed out my cereal bowl, and went back upstairs to get dressed." Note that the order of events is presented from the first event through the most recent event in the story. Both *cause and effect* and *chronology* help the reader to understand how or why events occurred.

<u>Example</u>

Identify the text structure that is used in the following sentence from *Charlie and the Chocolate Factory* by Roald Dahl:

> "'My dear sir!' cried Mr. Wonka, 'when I start selling this gum in the shops it will change everything!'"

The text structure of cause and effect is used in the sentence. The cause in the sentence is selling gum in the shops, and the effect is that everything will change. Information may also be organized according to chronological order, spatial order, order of importance, or organized by description. Chronological order means the order of events as they occur over time. Spatial order is the way things are placed in a location, such as the way people are seated around a table. Order of importance is used to place the most important information first, with the least important information last (or vice-versa). Description is used to organize information according to what it looks and feels like.

Procedural text

Procedural texts tell you how to accomplish a specific task. An example of this type of text is a recipe. The recipe will tell you what ingredients you need and all the information it will take to make the finished product. Another example of a procedural text is an instruction booklet that tells you how to put something together. Often procedural texts are accompanied by charts, diagrams, illustrations and graphs. These things help the reader to understand the information. Charts are used to list ingredients or parts that will be needed for the procedure. Diagrams are very helpful because they use pictures to show you how to complete a certain part of the procedure. Illustrations are helpful because they also can show you how something is supposed to look at steps along the way or a completed project. Graphs can also sometimes be used to show you information about other people's experiences with the same product or procedure.

Interpreting Graphical Information

A line graph is typically used for measuring trends over time. It is set up along a vertical and a horizontal axis. The variables being measured are listed along the left side and the bottom side of the axes. Points are then plotted along the graph, such that they correspond with their values for each variable. For instance, imagine a line graph measuring a person's income for each month of the year. If the person earned $1500 in January, there would be a point directly above January, perpendicular to the horizontal axis, and directly to the right of $1500, perpendicular to the vertical axis. Once all of the lines are plotted, they are connected with a line from left to right. This line provides a nice visual illustration of the general trends. For instance, using the earlier example, if the line sloped up, it would be clear that the person's income had increased over the course of the year.

The bar graph is one of the most common visual representations of information. Bar graphs are used to illustrate sets of numerical data. The graph has a vertical axis, along which numbers are listed, and a horizontal axis, along which categories, words, or some other indicators are placed. One example of a bar graph is a depiction of the respective heights of famous basketball players: the vertical axis would contain numbers ranging from five to eight feet, and the horizontal axis would contain the names of the players. The length of the bar above the player's name would illustrate his height, as the top of the bar would stop perpendicular to the height listed along the left side. In this representation, then, it would be easy to see that Yao Ming is taller than Michael Jordan, because Yao's bar would be higher.

A pie chart, also known as a circle graph, is useful for depicting how a single unit or category is divided. The standard pie chart is a circle within which wedges have been cut and labeled. Each of these wedges is proportional in size to its part of the whole. For instance, consider a pie chart representing a student's budget. If the student spends half her money on rent, then the pie chart will represent that amount with a line through the center of the pie. If she spends a quarter of her money on food, there will be a line extending from the edge of the circle to the center at a right angle to the line depicting rent. This illustration would make it clear that the student spends twice as much money on rent as she does on food. The pie chart is only appropriate for showing how a whole is divided.

Reading Practice Test #1

Practice Questions

Questions 1 – 13 pertain to the following story:

<u>The Tournament</u>

(1) The sun was warm as Keith and Joe walked home from school.

(2) "Tomorrow will be a perfect day to skateboard," Keith said. "Let's meet at the park at ten o'clock."

(3) "I can't," Joe said. "I have a karate tournament. I've been doing it since I was six."

(4) "Can't you get out of it?" Keith complained. "This will be the first sunny Saturday of spring."

(5) "I have a better idea. Come with me to the tournament." said Joe.

(6) "It sounds boring," Keith said.

(7) "It won't be boring," Joe promised. "Will you come?"

(8) "I'll ask my mom," Keith said.

(9) Later, Keith called Joe. "Mom said I can go. When will we meet?"

(10) "We'll pick you up at nine o'clock," Joe said. "See you tomorrow!"

(11) On the drive to the tournament, Joe told Keith that karate was a tradition in his family. Joe's father started studying karate when he was six, just like Joe. His grandfather learned karate as a boy in Okinawa.

(12) "Where's Okinawa?" Keith asked.

(13) "It's an island off the tip of Japan," Joe told him. "That's where my grandfather grew up."

(14) "Is your grandfather your karate teacher?" Keith asked.

(15) Joe laughed. "No. He's too old to teach anymore. I study with Master Lee in a dojo downtown."

(16) Joe explained that a dojo was a karate school. Master Lee taught many students in his dojo. In the tournament, Joe would compete against friends from his dojo and students from other dojos. He was nervous and excited.

(17) When they arrived at the tournament, Master Lee met them near the door. Joe introduced Keith to Master Lee. Master Lee smiled and bowed to Keith. Keith bowed back, even though he felt a little funny.

(18) Master Lee led them into the arena. The wide floor was divided into several rings. In each ring, students competed. Around the rings, family and friends cheered and offered encouragement. Joe waved to friends from his dojo.

(19) "I have to get dressed," Joe told Keith. "I'll be back in a few minutes."

(20) Joe disappeared into a locker room. When he came back, he wore a white top and pants. A green belt was tied around his waist.

(21) Keith grinned. "Nice outfit. Why is your belt green? It seems like everyone here has a different color of belt."

(22) Joe explained that belt color showed the skill level of a student. Beginners had white belts. After passing some tests, they earned a yellow belt. Then they earned a green belt. That was the skill level Joe had achieved. His next step was to earn a brown belt. Someday Joe hoped to earn a black belt like his father and grandfather and Master Lee. Then he could teach karate to others.

(23) Master Lee called Joe to a nearby ring. It was almost time for Joe to compete. He did some stretching exercises to prepare his body for competition. When Joe's name was called, he bowed to Master Lee and walked to the center of the ring.

(24) Keith felt worried. "What if he gets hurt?" Keith asked Joe's dad.

(25) Joe's dad explained it was a light contact competition. Students made only gentle, controlled contact with each other. They were judged on speed and accuracy rather than force or power. Keith was relieved.

(26) As the match began, Keith cheered for Joe as he punched, kicked, and blocked against his opponent's attacks. Joe was really good at karate! Keith and Joe's dad yelled and clapped as the match came to an end.

(27) Joe was breathless when he came to stand beside them. They waited anxiously for the judges' decision. The four judges conferred quietly at their table. Finally, they announced their decision: all four points went to Joe. Joe won the match!

(28) As the tournament continued, Joe kept winning matches. Keith cheered louder and louder with every win. He felt proud that someone as talented as Joe was his friend. He also admired the way his friend used his karate skills to honor his family's heritage. Keith hoped he could attend another tournament with Joe very soon!

1. In what season is the story set?
   a. Spring
   b. Summer
   c. Fall
   d. Winter

2. Why can't Joe go skateboarding with Keith?
   a. Joe hates skateboarding
   b. Joe has a class at Master Lee's dojo
   c. Joe has to go to a karate tournament
   d. Joe doesn't like Keith anymore

3. What is a dojo?
   a. A karate technique
   b. A karate school
   c. A karate teacher
   d. A karate student

4. According to the story, what does a karate student's belt color represent?
   a. The student's favorite color
   b. The student's karate teacher
   c. The form of karate the student studies
   d. The student's skill level

5. In paragraph 27, what is the definition of the word "conferred"?
   a. Argued
   b. Joked
   c. Decided
   d. Discussed

6. Based on the story, why does Joe want Keith to come to the karate tournament with him?
   a. Joe wants Keith to understand that karate is important to him
   b. Joe does not want Keith to go skateboarding without him
   c. Joe wants Keith to meet Master Lee and Joe's dad
   d. Joe wants Keith to be jealous of his karate skills

7. What point of view is used to tell this story?
   a. First person
   b. Second person
   c. Third person
   d. All of the above

8. Which of the following best describes how Keith's attitude toward the karate tournament changes between paragraph 6 and paragraph 28?
   a. Keith's attitude does not change at all
   b. Keith goes from thinking the tournament is boring to hoping to attend another one
   c. Keith goes from thinking that karate is an awesome sport to thinking that karate is boring
   d. Keith decides he doesn't want to skateboard anymore; he wants to study karate

9. Complete the following chart based on information in the story:
White belt
Yellow belt

____

Brown belt
Black belt

    a. Blue belt
    b. Green belt
    c. Red belt
    d. Purple belt

10. What is the primary purpose of this story?
    a. To show how important karate is to Joe
    b. To show how much Keith likes skateboarding
    c. To show how long Keith and Joe have been friends
    d. To show what a good teacher Master Lee is

11. Based on the information given in the story, how likely is Joe to keep practicing karate?
    a. Very unlikely
    b. Somewhat unlikely
    c. Somewhat likely
    d. Very likely

12. Which of the following statements about the story is a fact, rather than an opinion?
    a. By the end of the story, Keith wants to take karate
    b. Because Joe wins all his matches, Master Lee is obviously an excellent teacher
    c. Joe's father and grandfather both practice karate
    d. None of the other students in Master Lee's dojo are as good as Joe

13. Based on the story, how does practicing karate honor Joe's family heritage?
    a. Karate is taught in Okinawa, and Joe's grandfather is Okinawan
    b. Karate is a tradition in Joe's family, practiced by three generations
    c. Karate is popular in the town where Joe and his family live
    d. Many Asians practice karate, and Joe is Asian

Remember the Alamo

(1) In the early 1700s, the Spanish established missions throughout the land we now know as the state of Texas. One of the most famous of these missions was San Antonio de Valero, better known by its nickname: the Alamo. This was the most successful mission in the area, and it served a number of purposes for the surrounding communities.

(2) For over a century, the Alamo served as an active mission. Church services were held in the cool, shady buildings, providing welcome relief from the blazing summer sun. Couples were married at the Alamo. Babies were baptized there. The Alamo also served as a trading post, supply depot, and communication center. In later years, however, the Alamo served its most famous and—arguably—most important role; it was a fortress for freedom fighters.

(3) During the 1830s, Texas was in a battle for independence from Mexico, which owned it at that time. This struggle came to a head in 1836 when 184 Texans, led by William Travis, holed up in the Alamo. Travis and other famous American fighters— including Jim Bowie and Davy Crockett—fought side by side with farmers, ranchers, cowboys, and businessmen. Those brave men held off Mexican General Santa Anna's army for 13 days from the secure walls of the Alamo.

(4) Finally, in the gray, early morning light of March 6, 1836, General Santa Anna and an army of 4,000 soldiers overran the Alamo. Every man in the Alamo died that day, but their ability to hold out for nearly two weeks gave American General Sam Houston the time he needed to assemble a more substantial army. General Houston soon defeated General Santa Anna, and Texas won its independence, thanks in great part to the brave men who defended the Alamo and the cause of freedom.

A Day at the Alamo

(1) Just before spring break, Eric's class took a trip to visit the Alamo. Before they left, they read about William Travis, Jim Bowie, and Davy Crockett in their history books. They also read about General Santa Anna and his army. Eric couldn't wait to see the place where the actual battle for the Alamo occurred.

(2) Eric watched buildings roll by as the school bus drove into downtown San Antonio. Near the River Walk, the bus stopped and the class climbed out.

(3) "Stay together, please," Mrs. Morgan, Eric's teacher, directed the class. "After I check us in, we will go listen to a history talk."

(4) A few minutes later, Mrs. Morgan led the class to a patio area. A guide met them there and told the story of the Alamo, from its establishment by the Spanish to the famous standoff and battle in 1836. Eric listened carefully. He wanted to remember all the details to help him complete the History Hunt worksheet Mrs. Morgan had given them.

(5) When the history talk was over, Mrs. Morgan divided the class into small groups. Each group was assigned a parent volunteer and given an hour to complete a self-tour of the Alamo and the grounds. During that time, they were supposed to look for all the necessary answers to complete their History Hunt worksheets. In an hour, all groups would meet at the gift shop.

(6) Eric loved walking through the old buildings and viewing the artifacts. He liked the gardens and the Long Barrack Museum, but his favorite building was the Shrine. He especially liked the old bell that was kept in a small room in the Shrine. Eric could imagine Davy Crockett himself ringing that bell!

(7) Soon the hour was up, and Eric's group headed for the gift shop. While there, Eric used his allowance to buy a book about Davy Crockett and a small Texas flag. Back on the bus, Eric waved his flag proudly at passing cars. He knew he would always remember the Alamo.

Use the story "Remember the Alamo" to answer questions 14–19

14. What was the official name of the mission nicknamed "the Alamo"?

    a. San Antonio de Valente
    b. San Antonio de Verde
    c. San Antonio de Valero
    d. San Antonio de Vallejo

15. Which of the following represents the author's main purpose in writing this story?

    a. To inform
    b. To influence
    c. To entertain
    d. To persuade

16. What was the main motivation for the men who fought at the Alamo?

    a. Wealth
    b. Fame
    c. Safety
    d. Freedom

17. Based on the information in paragraph 2, what was the purpose of the Alamo?

    a. It was designed as a war fortress
    b. It was designed to serve many purposes in the community
    c. It was designed as a trading post
    d. It was designed as a saloon

18. Which of the following is a statement of opinion?

    a. William Travis, Davy Crockett, and Jim Bowie fought at the Alamo
    b. All the men who fought to defend the Alamo died in the battle
    c. General Santa Anna was eventually defeated by General Sam Houston
    d. General Santa Anna was a better leader than William Travis

19. How many Americans died while defending the Alamo?

    a. 184
    b. 13
    c. 136
    d. 47

Use the story "A Day at the Alamo" to answer questions 20–25

20. Where does the story say the Alamo is located?

    a. Just outside San Antonio
    b. Near the San Antonio River
    c. In downtown San Antonio
    d. Across the river from San Antonio

21. Which artifact was Eric's favorite during his trip to the Alamo?

    a. The Texas flag
    b. The old bell
    c. The Long Barrack Museum
    d. The gardens

22. Complete the following schedule for Eric's class trip:

1. Arrive at the Alamo and check in
2. Attend history talk on the patio
3. Divide into groups for self-tour
4. _______________________

    a. Meet in the gardens
    b. Meet on the patio
    c. Meet at the gift shop
    d. Meet at the bus

23. Why was Eric so excited about visiting the Alamo?

    a. He wanted to see where the battle occurred
    b. He heard there were interesting items in the gift shop
    c. He enjoyed riding on the school bus
    d. His friends were excited about the trip

24. In paragraph 6, what is the best definition of the word "artifacts"?
   a. Buildings
   b. Historical items
   c. Documents and pictures
   d. Furnishings

25. Which paragraph tells the most about Eric's favorite experiences at the Alamo?
   a. Paragraph 4
   b. Paragraph 5
   c. Paragraph 6
   d. Paragraph 7

Use both "Remember the Alamo" and "A Day at the Alamo" to answer questions 26 and 27.

26. What theme is central to both of these stories, joining them together?
   a. Love of freedom
   b. Davy Crockett
   c. Independence of Texas
   d. History of the Alamo

27. Which of the following represents the biggest difference between the stories?
   a. One involves a school class and the other doesn't
   b. The Alamo changed a lot between the two stories
   c. One is nonfiction and the other is fiction
   d. One involves General Santa Anna and the other doesn't

Questions 28-40 pertain to the following passage:

A Lesson Learned

(1) Beautiful melodies floated from Uncle Eddie's guitar. Kari listened with wonder. The way Uncle Eddie made the guitar sing filled Kari with a desire to learn to play. She wanted to make beautiful music too.

(2) "Teach me to play, Uncle Eddie," Kari begged.

(3) Uncle Eddie looked intently at Kari. "Learning to play isn't easy, Kari. It takes hard work and practice. Are you ready for that?"

(4) "I am! I promise." Kari was thrilled. She was sure playing the guitar would come easily for her. "When can we start?"

(5) "I'll come by at two o'clock on Saturday," Uncle Eddie said. "Be ready to work hard."

(6) Kari laughed. "I will," she promised. "Thanks, Uncle Eddie. See you Saturday!"

(7) Kari could hardly wait for Saturday to come. She dreamed about the songs she would play. She imagined impressing her friends with her skills. Kari was sure she would be a guitar expert in no time. She was so excited.

(8) On Saturday afternoon, Uncle Eddie rang the doorbell. Kari ran to let him in.

(9) "Ready to learn?" Uncle Eddie greeted her.

(10) Kari nodded. She followed him into the family room. She waited for him to get out his guitar and teach her a song, but he didn't even open the case. Instead, he took a book from his music bag.

(11) "We'll start with a history of the guitar," Uncle Eddie said. "Did you know stringed instruments have been around for thousands of years?"

(12) Kari was unimpressed. "Wow," she said.

(13) Uncle Eddie said guitars came from Spain more than 500 years ago. He said they could be used to play a variety of music styles and were one of the most popular instruments.

(14) Kari sighed. "That's great, Uncle Eddie, but I just want to play. When can I start playing songs?"

(15) Uncle Eddie laughed. "Patience, Kari. There's a lot to learn about the guitar before you're ready to play one."

(16) "Like what?" Kari asked.

(17) Uncle Eddie handed her a diagram of a guitar. He explained the two basic guitar parts were the body and the neck. These were made up of other parts.

(18) "The tuning pegs are tightened and loosened so the strings make the right notes," Uncle Eddie told Kari.

(19) Then he showed her the nut at the top and the bridge at the bottom that held the strings in place. He pointed out the fingerboard all along the neck and the frets that helped with finger placement. Finally, he described the top of the body—the sounding board—with a hole in the middle to produce a sweet sound.

(20) Uncle Eddie told Kari to learn the names of the guitar parts as her homework for the next lesson.

(21) "But I don't want homework," Kari protested. "I want to play songs! I didn't even play one note."

(22) With a sigh, Uncle Eddie opened his guitar case and took out his instrument. He played a simple folk song. When he played the song three times, Kari grinned.

(23) "I've got it! I can do this," Kari insisted.

(24) Uncle Eddie showed her how to hold the guitar. Kari started to play, but the notes were all wrong. It didn't sound at all like Uncle Eddie's beautiful music. Kari handed the guitar back to Uncle Eddie with frustration.

(25) "Maybe the guitar isn't for me," she said.

(26) Without a word, Uncle Eddie took out a CD and put it in the player behind him. Tuneless, horrible music filled the room. Kari laughed.

(27) "Hey! That person is worse than I am," she said.

(28) Uncle Eddie smiled. "That's me at my first lesson."

(29) "No way!" Kari said.

(30) "Yep," said Uncle Eddie. "Kari, I've played for 15 years. It took time and practice to get this good."

(31) "Do you think I could play like you someday?" Kari asked.

(32) "If you work hard," answered Uncle Eddie.

(33) "Maybe I should start with my homework for our next lesson," Kari said.

(34) Uncle Eddie hugged her. "That sounds like a great place to start."

28. What is the setting for Kari's guitar lessons?
    a. Uncle Eddie's house
    b. Kari's house
    c. A music school
    d. The community center

29. Based on the story, which of the following best qualifies Uncle Eddie to teach guitar lessons to Kari?
    a. He is Kari's uncle
    b. He has taught many guitar students before
    c. He is looking for work
    d. He knows how to play the guitar very well

30. Which part of the guitar is used to help strings make the right notes?
    a. Tuning pegs
    b. Fingerboard
    c. Bridge
    d. Soundboard

31. When did Uncle Eddie say he would come to give Kari her first guitar lesson?

    a. Friday at two o'clock
    b. Saturday at noon
    c. Saturday at two o'clock
    d. Sunday at noon

32. In paragraph 3, what does the word "intently" mean?

    a. In a focused way
    b. In a disinterested way
    c. In a happy way
    d. In a disgusted way

33. Which of the following belongs in the empty box according to the sequence of the story?

Kari wants to learn to play the guitar.	Uncle Eddie agrees to teach her.		Kari becomes bored and frustrated.	Kari learns it takes hard work to play guitar.

    a. Kari plays well on her first try
    b. Uncle Eddie begins the lesson with the history and structure of the guitar
    c. Uncle Eddie does not show up for the lesson
    d. Kari's friends decide they want Uncle Eddie to teach them too

34. What is the main theme of this story?

    a. To show that Uncle Eddie is not a good teacher
    b. To show that Kari is not a good student
    c. To show that learning to play the guitar is boring
    d. To show that learning to play the guitar takes hard work

35. In what point of view is this story written?

    a. First person
    b. Second person
    c. Third person
    d. All of the above

36. What is the difference between Uncle Eddie's feelings and Kari's feelings about learning to play the guitar?

    a. Uncle Eddie feels it will be hard, while Kari feels it will be easy
    b. Kari feels it will be hard, while Uncle Eddie feels it will be easy
    c. Both Kari and Uncle Eddie feel it will be hard
    d. Both Kari and Uncle Eddie feel it will be easy

37. How does the author show in paragraph 14 that Kari is unhappy with Uncle Eddie's history lesson on guitars?

    a. By saying, "Kari was unhappy."
    b. By having Kari say something unkind to Uncle Eddie
    c. By writing, "Kari sighed."
    d. By having Kari leave the room

38. Who is playing the "horrible music" Kari hears in paragraph 26?
    a. Uncle Eddie's first student
    b. Uncle Eddie
    c. Kari
    d. Kari's father

39. Based on what was discussed in the story, what does it take to play the guitar well?
    a. A very expensive guitar
    b. A very skilled guitar teacher
    c. A thorough knowledge of guitar history
    d. Hard work and a lot of practice

40. Based on the information presented in the story, which of the following is a fact instead of an opinion?
    a. Uncle Eddie has been playing guitar for 15 years
    b. Kari will never learn to be a good guitar player
    c. Playing the guitar is a boring hobby
    d. Everyone who plays the guitar knows a lot about guitar history

Answers and Explanations

TEKS Standard §110.15(b)(6)

1. A: In paragraph 4, Keith tells Joe that tomorrow will be a great day for skateboarding because it will be the first sunny Saturday of spring.

TEKS Standard §110.15(b)(6)

2. C: In paragraph 3 Joe tells Keith that he can't go skateboarding because he has a tournament to attend.

TEKS Standard §110.15(b)(6)

3. B: In paragraph 16, Joe explains to Keith that a dojo is a karate school.

TEKS Standard §110.15(b)(6)

4. D: In paragraph 21, Keith mentions to Joe that there are many different colors of belts being worn. In the next paragraph, Joe explains that the different colors represent the level of karate skill each person possesses.

TEKS Standard §110.15(b)(2)(B)

5. D: The correct definition of "conferred" is "discussed." If you didn't know what the word meant before reading the story, you could use the context and the answer choices to help you understand the word. The judges had come together to make their decision about scoring. They weren't having an argument, and they weren't joking. Deciding is what they did *after* they conferred. So "discussed" is really the only answer that fits.

TEKS Standard §110.15(b)(6)

6. A: The story makes it clear that karate is a very important part of Joe's life. His father studied karate, and so did his grandfather. Joe has been studying it since he was six years old. Since Keith is a close friend, Joe wanted to share this important part of his life with him.

TEKS Standard §110.15(b)(6)(C)

7. C: This story is written from the third person point of view. That means it is being told by a *narrator*, that is, someone who doesn't appear in the story. If Joe were telling the story, it would be the first person point of view. Second person point of view is used when a person writes or talks to another person, addressing them as "you", or by their name.

TEKS Standard §110.15(b)(6)(B)

8. B: In paragraph 6, after Joe first invites him to attend the karate tournament, Keith says it sounds boring. By the end of the story, his attitude had completely changed. Far from being bored, he was fascinated with karate, and couldn't wait to attend another tournament.

TEKS Standard §110.15(b)(6)

9. B: In paragraph 22, Joe explains what the differently colored belts mean. A white belt is for beginners, while a student who has made some progress earns a yellow belt. The next highest belt is green, followed by brown. The black belt is the final color, and it's for experts. So green is the missing color.

TEKS Standard §110.15(b)(3)(A)

10. A: The primary purpose of the story is to show that karate is important to Joe. The other answers are things we also learn from the story, but none of them are the main point of the story.

TEKS Standard §110.15(b)(6)(A)

11. D: It's obvious that karate is very important to Joe, so he is very likely to keep practicing it.

TEKS Standard §110.15(b)(11)(B)

12. C: is the best choice because the story states as facts that Joe's father and grandfather both practice karate. By the end of the story, Keith has decided that karate isn't boring, but the author doesn't say that he wants to start taking lessons. Since Joe wins all his matches, Master Lee is probably an excellent teacher, but there could be other explanations for Joe's success. The story says that Joe won the tournament, but that doesn't necessarily mean he's the best in his class.

TEKS Standard §110.15(b)(6)

13. B: is the best choice because karate is part of Joe's family heritage, as three generations of his family practice karate. The other answer choices reflect Joe's national and community heritages, but only B is about his family heritage.

TEKS Standard §110.15(b)(11)

14. C: We learn in the first paragraph that "the Alamo" is a nickname, and the full name of the mission is San Antonio de Valero.

TEKS Standard §110.15(b)(11)(A)

15. A: The author's purpose in writing "Remember the Alamo" is to inform. He is presenting information, or facts, about the Alamo.

TEKS Standard §110.15(b)(11)

16. D: At the time of the Battle of the Alamo, the people of Texas were fighting to become independent of Mexico. They wanted to be free of Mexican rule to pursue their own destiny.

TEKS Standard §110.15(b)(11)

17. B: Paragraph 1 informs us that the Alamo served many purposes in the community, and Paragraph 2 tells us what some of those purposes were.

TEKS Standard §110.15(b)(11)(B)

18. D: The first three answer choices are actual facts which are stated in the piece, but D represents an opinion, one that many people would disagree with.

TEKS Standard §110.15(b)(11)

19. A: Paragraph 3 tells us that there were 184 men at the Alamo. In Paragraph 4 we learn that all the men in the Alamo died during the battle.

TEKS Standard §110.15(b)(6)

20. C: In paragraph 2 we learn that the Alamo is in downtown San Antonio.

TEKS Standard §110.15(b)(6)

21. B: We learn in Paragraph 6 that Eric like the old bell the best.

TEKS Standard §110.15(b)(6)(A)

22. C: This answer is found in Paragraph 5.

TEKS Standard §110.15(b)(6)

23. A: This answer is found in Paragraph 1.

TEKS Standard §110.15(b)(6)

24. B: The best definition for the word "artifacts" is "historical items".

TEKS Standard §110.15(b)(2)(B)

25. C: Paragraph 6 describes Eric's favorite experiences at the Alamo. In the other paragraphs we learn facts about his visit, but only this one tells us what his favorite experiences were.

TEKS Standard §110.15(b)(3)(A) and (11)(A)

26. D: is the best choice because the two stories both have a central theme of the history of the Alamo, linking them together. While A, B, and C are mentioned in both stories, they are not the best choices because they do not represent central themes in the stories.

TEKS Standard §110.15(b)(3)

27. C: The biggest difference between the two stories is that one is nonfiction and the other is fiction. The first story is non-fiction, and the second one is fiction.

TEKS Standard §110.15(b)(6)

28. B: The story indicates that the setting is Kari's house, although it never actually says so. In Paragraph 5, Uncle Eddie tells her he'll come by on Saturday. In Paragraph 8, he rang the doorbell and Kari let him in. These two paragraphs make it clear that the setting is Kari's house.

TEKS Standard §110.15(b)(6)

29. D: Based on the story, Uncle Eddie is qualified to teach guitar because he plays very well. If Uncle Eddie had taught many other students how to play guitar before teaching Kari, that would also be a reason he is qualified to teach her. However, there is nothing in the story that indicates that he has ever taught anyone else how to play before this.

- 45 -

TEKS Standard §110.15(b)(6)

30. A: is the best choice because the tuning pegs of a guitar are used to help the strings make the right note. B, C, and D are not the best choices because they are not used to help tune the guitar.

TEKS Standard §110.15(b)(6)

31. C: This answer is found in paragraph 5.

TEKS Standard §110.15(b)(2)(B)

32. A: The word "intently" means "in a focused way." If you didn't know this word, you could use the context to help you understand the meaning.

TEKS Standard §110.15(b)(6)(A)

33. B: You want to pick the box that shows what happened after Uncle Eddie agrees to teach Kari, but before Kari started getting bored. The only box that fits is B, which mentions Uncle Eddie's lesson on the history of the guitar (which is why Kari was getting bored.)

TEKS Standard §110.15(b)(3)(A)

34. D: The main theme of the story is to show that learning to play the guitar takes hard work.

TEKS Standard §110.15(b)(6)(C)

35. C: This story is written in the third person. That means it's told by someone who isn't part of the story, called a *narrator*.

TEKS Standard §110.15(b)(6)

36. A: Uncle Eddie feels playing the guitar will be hard, but Kari feels it will be easy. As the story goes on, Kari learns how wrong she was, and discovers that Uncle Eddie was right – learning to play the guitar takes a lot of hard work.

TEKS Standard §110.15(b)(6)

37. C: Paragraph 14 says "Kari sighed" as the author's way of indicating Kari's displeasure. A, B, and D are not the best choices because they do not reference details included in paragraph 14.

TEKS Standard §110.15(b)(6)

38. B: Uncle Eddie is playing the "horrible music" Kari hears in paragraph 26. This is one of the turning points of the story, because when Kari realizes that Uncle Eddie used to be a terrible guitar player, she decides that she shouldn't give up just because it's hard.

TEKS Standard §110.15(b)(6)

39. D: is the best choice because the story points out that it takes a lot of practice and hard work to play the guitar well. A, B, and C represent things that might be helpful in learning to play the guitar, but the main requirements are hard work and lots of practice.

- 46 -

40. A: This answer is the only statement of fact from the story.

Reading Practice Test #2

Practice Questions

Questions 1 – 13 pertain to the following passage:

<u>That Was Then, and This Is Now</u>

(1) Becca slumped on Grandma's flowered sofa. She loved Grandma, but her house was so dull. Becca was bored.

(2) "Grandma, there's nothing to do!" Becca whined.

(3) "You could watch TV," Grandma suggested.

(4) "There's nothing to watch on your channels. Why don't you have cable?" Becca asked.

(5) "I don't need cable," Grandma said. "When I was little, there were only three television stations available. In fact, we didn't even have a TV until I was 12 years old. And even then, it was black-and-white."

(6) "That sounds awful," Becca said.

(7) "Actually, we thought it was wonderful," Grandma said. "But that was then, and this is now."

(8) "Well, what about getting a game system or a computer. That would give me something to do when I'm here," Becca said.

(9) "We didn't have computers or game systems when I was young," Grandma said. "But we always managed to keep ourselves quite busy."

(10) "You must have been so bored all the time," Becca said. "What did you do to keep busy?"

(11) "Oh, we played outside. We rode our bikes, and sometimes we stuck playing cards in the spokes of the wheels to make them sound like motorcycles. We went fishing and built forts out of blankets or scrap wood or whatever else we could find. Yes, we kept busy." Grandma smiled, remembering.

(12) "I guess that doesn't sound so bad," Becca said. "But what if it was raining, like today? Then you couldn't do any of those things."

(13) "On rainy days, we played inside games," Grandma said. "We played checkers and solitaire and other games. We read books for hours. We made paper dolls and designed whole wardrobes for them. But I guess that was then, and this is now."

(14) "Wow," said Becca. "That sounds kind of fun. What else was different way back then?"

(15) Grandma laughed. "It wasn't all that long ago, Becca. But many things were different."

(16) Grandma told Becca about having fresh milk delivered to her doorstep in glass bottles instead of buying it in plastic jugs at the supermarket. She talked about wearing dresses to school every day instead of jeans and T-shirts. She talked about using pay phones instead of cell phones. She talked about listening to soap operas on the radio instead of watching them on TV. She talked about playing records and dancing the twist.

(17) "But that was then," Grandma said, "and this is now."

(18) Becca was amazed. "You're right, Grandma. Practically everything is different now. It seems like the whole world has changed since you were my age."

(19) Grandma shook her head. "Not everything has changed, Becca. Some things will never change."

(20) "Like what?" Becca asked.

(21) "Well," Grandma answered, "back then grandmas loved their granddaughters, just like I love you now."

(22) Becca leaned over and hugged Grandma tightly. "I love you, too," she said. "Now, how about a game of checkers?"

(23) Grandma smiled. "Sounds good. Maybe things haven't changed so much after all!"

(24) They played checkers, and Grandma beat Becca all three games. Then they used pillows and blankets and all six dining room chairs to build a massive fort in the living room. They sat in the dim fort and had a picnic lunch of sandwiches and chocolate chip cookies. After lunch, Grandma showed Becca how to make paper dolls and design clothes for them. The afternoon flew past.

(25) When Becca's mom came to pick her up, Becca did not want to go home.

(26) "But I thought you were bored," Grandma said.

(27) Becca grinned. "Oh, Grandma," she said, "I was bored. But that was then, and this is now!"

1. Where does this story take place?
   a. At Becca's house
   b. At Grandma's house
   c. At a vacation house
   d. At Becca's mom's house

2. Which of the following best represents the main theme of this story?

   a. There are many different ways to have fun
   b. Becca is bored all the time
   c. Grandma is old and dull
   d. Activities from the past are not exciting

3. How does Becca feel at the beginning of this story?

   a. Happy
   b. Sad
   c. Angry
   d. Bored

4. What word does the author use in paragraph 1 to describe Becca's feelings about Grandma's house?

   a. Exciting
   b. Tolerable
   c. Dull
   d. Boring

5. What is the difference between Becca's attitude at the beginning of the story and her attitude at the end?

   a. There is no difference in her attitude
   b. She is bored at the beginning of the story and not bored at the end
   c. She is angry with Grandma at the beginning of the story and happy with her at the end
   d. She is excited at the beginning of the story and bored at the end

6. Which of the following does the story say Grandma did to keep busy when she was young?

   a. Watch color TV
   b. Use a computer
   c. Play outside
   d. Go to the mall

7. What point of view does the author use to tell this story?

   a. First person
   b. Second person
   c. Third person
   d. All of the above

8. What is the author's main purpose in writing this story?

   a. To entertain
   b. To inform
   c. To persuade
   d. To influence

9. Which of the following is a statement of fact?

   a. Black-and-white TV is boring
   b. Grandma is a dull person
   c. Milk used to be delivered in glass bottles
   d. Playing outside is exciting

10. Where do Grandma and Becca eat their lunch in this story?

    a. Outside on the lawn
    b. In a blanket fort
    c. At the dining table
    d. At a restaurant

11. Which of the following does Becca ask Grandma to get in this story?

    a. A dog
    b. A TV
    c. A car
    d. A computer

12. Which character in this story has the more positive attitude?

    a. Becca
    b. Grandma
    c. Becca's mom
    d. No one in the story has a positive attitude

13. Which paragraph is the first to show a definite change in Becca's attitude?

    a. Paragraph 10
    b. Paragraph 22
    c. Paragraph 24
    d. Paragraph 26

Questions 14 – 27 pertain to the passages:

The Tradition of Dance

(1) It is estimated that there are over 300 Native American tribes, and each of them uses dancing to communicate culture. Native American dances date back hundreds of years and come in many different forms. Different tribes use dance for different purposes and to convey different messages.

(2) Although each dance is different, they all have meanings that are rooted in ancient tradition. The Iroquois performed a corn husk dance to bring good crops and many healthy babies to the tribe. The Choctaw women danced with medicine men to bring their tribe victory in sporting events. The Plains Indians offered thanks to the gods through their Sun Dance, and the Cherokee celebrated both peace and war with the Eagle Dance. During the Snake Ceremonial, Hopi dancers even held live snakes in their mouths before releasing them into the desert to bring rain and a good harvest.

(3) Each of the many different dances also requires a unique costume. These costumes vary widely, but—just like the dances—each has a special meaning. Most dance costumes include a headdress and special ceremonial clothing. Some also include a wand, jewelry, and even body paint. In addition, feathers are often used in costumes to symbolize human traits. One of the most common feathers used is the eagle feather, which represents strength in many tribes.

(4) Though many of the Native American dances are now performed only in ceremonies and at powwows, they remain an important element of Native American

culture. These dances are a language, rich in history and meaning. They are passed from generation to generation and will always be a vital part of Native American tradition.

The Story of My People

(1) As we pulled into the community college parking lot, I felt my excitement rising. Powwows were one of my favorite things. I loved the talking, the laughing, the music, and—most of all—the dancing. I loved seeing and hearing and feeling my Cherokee heritage.

(2) Inside the large gymnasium, the powwow was just getting started. My father and grandfather went to join the men who had gathered in the far corner. Around the edges of the gym, women sat behind long tables draped with vibrant cloths. On the tables were items for sale. I wandered around and looked at the leather vests, beaded belts, and beautiful jewelry.

(3) As I came to the end of the tables, I heard behind me the low, pulsing beat of a single drum. It made a hollow, echoing sound. Soon other drums joined the rhythm, filling the air with their deep sound. High-pitched rattles joined in, and a group of men drifted to the center of the floor. The dancing had begun.

(4) I found a seat on some bleachers and watched with wonder. Synchronized steps beat out a perfect rhythm while voices chanted high and low in beautiful unison. Feathers and beads and shiny black braids flashed past as the intensity increased. It was magical to me.

(5) Some dances were for the children; some were for the men or women; some were for everyone. Sometimes tribes danced separately, and sometimes they all danced together. Some dances offered thanks, and others asked for blessings; some were celebrations, and others were prayers. But although each dance was different, they all told a story. It was an ancient story: the story of my people.

Questions 14 -1 19 pertain to the passage "The Tradition of Dance":
14. According to the article, how many Native American tribes are there?
    a. Over 500
    b. Over 100
    c. Over 300
    d. Over 700

15. What is the main purpose of dance in the Native American culture?
    a. To provide exercise
    b. To communicate a message
    c. To entertain children
    d. To prepare for battle

16. According to paragraph 2, what is the similarity between the Iroquois corn husk dance and the Hopi Snake Ceremonial?

    a. They were both intended to bring good crops
    b. They both involved women and medicine men
    c. They both involved the use of snakes
    d. They both involved the use of corn husks

17. Which of the following is a statement of fact?

    a. Eagle feathers are the best feathers
    b. Native American costumes are beautiful
    c. Ceremonial headdresses make dancers look important
    d. Many Native American costumes include a wand and jewelry

18. What does the eagle feather represent in many Native American tribes?

    a. Power
    b. Wealth
    c. Strength
    d. Authority

19. What was the author's main purpose in writing this article?

    a. To inform
    b. To entertain
    c. To influence
    d. To persuade

Questions 20 – 25 pertain to the passage: "The Story of My People"
20. What tribe represents the heritage of the narrator of this story?

    a. Hopi
    b. Cherokee
    c. Iroquois
    d. Choctaw

21. In what point of view is this story written?

    a. First person
    b. Second person
    c. Third person
    d. None of the above

22. What is the primary reason the narrator enjoys going to powwows so much?

    a. They are very exciting
    b. There are many people there
    c. There are interesting things to buy
    d. They represent the narrator's heritage

23. What is the main theme of this story?

    a. Native American dancing tells a story
    b. Powwows are exciting
    c. Community colleges are great places to hold powwows
    d. Native American children learn to dance at a young age

24. Which of the following is a statement of opinion?
    a. Some dances are designed to bring a blessing
    b. Each dance is different, but each has a meaning
    c. Many dances involve synchronized steps, music, and chanting
    d. Native American dancing is emotionally powerful

25. What does the narrator do before the dancing begins?
    a. Buys snacks at the snack bar
    b. Looks at the tables of items for sale
    c. Takes a walk around the campus
    d. Practices different dancing steps

Questions 26 – 27 pertain to both passages "The Tradition of Dance" and "The Story of My People"

26. What main theme is central to both stories?
    a. The value of powwows in Native American culture
    b. The focus on family in Native American culture
    c. The importance of dancing in Native American culture
    d. The power of medicine men in Native American culture

27. What is Native American dancing compared to in both stories?
    a. Language
    b. Music
    c. Cooking
    d. Art

Questions 28 – 40 pertain to the following passage:

<u>In Abuela's World</u>

(1) In June, just after school ended, Marianna and her family went to see her abuela—her grandmother—in Tampico, Mexico. By the time they reached Abuela's small house by the sea, Marianna was exhausted. Abuela put a thick mat on the floor for a bed, and Marianna stretched out and went to sleep.

(2) When Marianna awoke the next morning, the sun was already high in the sky. The air was warm and sticky. Marianna rubbed her eyes and wandered into Abuela's kitchen. Delicious smells bubbled up from a pot on the stove.

(3) "Buenos dias, sleepyhead," Abuela said with a grin. "You must have been tired. You slept half the day away."

(4) Marianna stretched and yawned as her mother came into the kitchen. "What are we doing today, Mami?" Marianna asked.

(5) "Papi and Jorge and I are going down to the beach soon," Mami answered. "You can come with us or stay here with Abuela."

(6) Marianna chose the beach. As she lay in the sun, she listened to the waves. Sea birds called overhead, and the gentle sea breeze kissed her face. It was a perfect afternoon.

(7) The next day, Abuela joined them as they drove south to visit some Aztec ruins. Although the Aztec people once ruled the area of Mexico where Abuela lived, they were conquered by the Spaniards long ago. Crumbling ruins were all that remained of their ancient civilization. Marianna had read about the Aztecs in school. It was amazing to think these stones were once part of the great Aztec empire.

(8) On her third full day in Mexico, Marianna saw her cousins. The three boys shyly greeted Marianna. Then they turned to her younger brother, Jorge.

(9) "Want to play some futbol, Jorge?" they asked.

(10) Jorge nodded. He knew futbol meant soccer in Spanish, and he loved soccer. Marianna went out to watch the boys play. She liked soccer, too, but it was too hot to play in the blazing sun.

(11) Marianna sat on the shady porch and watched the boys kick the ball in the dusty street. The boys played hard, and Marianna found herself cheering for Jorge's team. As the sun went down, they called it a tie and finally headed inside.

(12) The visit to Abuela's world flew by. On the day before she had to leave, Marianna found Abuela in the kitchen.

(13) "I don't want to go home," Marianna said. "I love you, and I love Mexico."

(14) Abuela smiled. "I love you, too. But you would eventually miss your life in America. And you can always come to visit."

(15) "I guess so," said Marianna. "But I'll miss Mexico."

(16) "I know," said Abuela, taking Marianna's hand. "So to help you take Mexico with you, we are having a grand fiesta tonight. Come shopping with me."

(17) They went to the open market where vendors spread their goods on blankets on the ground. Abuela selected items for the party, greeting many of the vendors by name. Then she bought Marianna some chicle, Mexican gum made from sapodilla pulp.

(18) That night, dozens of neighbors, friends, and family members came to the party. They talked and laughed and danced to the mariachi music. Abuela made incredible food for everyone. There was chicken with sweet and spicy mole, enchiladas with rich sauce, rice, fruit, and plenty of tortillas. It was a true feast.

(19) The party went late into the night. Marianna felt she had barely slept when Papi shook her awake and told her it was time to go. As they drove away, Marianna waved to Abuela. Although she was going home, Marianna knew her heart would always hold a special place for Abuela's world.

28. What is the Spanish word for grandmother?
   a. Amiga
   b. Abuela
   c. Alla
   d. Alegra

29. Where is the main setting for this story?

    a. In the southwest
    b. In Tampico, Mexico
    c. At the ruins
    d. In the open market

30. What kind of ruins does Marianna's family visit?

    a. Aztec ruins
    b. Mayan ruins
    c. Navajo ruins
    d. Spaniard ruins

31. Which choice best finishes the following chart of events on Marianna's vacation?

Marianna goes to the beach.	Marianna visits the ruins.	Marianna sees her cousins.	Marianna visits the open market.	

    a. Marianna visits a mountain
    b. Marianna takes a road trip through Mexico
    c. Marianna attends a big party at her grandmother's house
    d. Marianna watches the boys play soccer

32. Which paragraphs discuss Marianna's visit with her cousins?

    a. Paragraph 5 through paragraph 9
    b. Paragraph 6 through paragraph 10
    c. Paragraph 7 through paragraph 10
    d. Paragraph 8 through paragraph 11

33. Which word is the best English translation for the Spanish word "futbol"?

    a. Football
    b. Soccer
    c. Baseball
    d. Kickball

34. Why did the author tell this story from Marianna's point of view?

    a. So the reader can understand Marianna's thoughts and feelings
    b. Because there was no other main character in the story
    c. Because all good stories are written in third-person point of view
    d. This story is not written from Marianna's point of view

35. Why does the story say Marianna doesn't want to leave Mexico?

    a. She hates the long trip
    b. She doesn't have to go to school in Mexico
    c. She loves her grandmother, and she loves Mexico
    d. She likes the weather at the beach

36. In paragraph 6, which literary device is used to describe the wind?

    a. Simile
    b. Personification
    c. Metaphor
    d. No literary device is used

37. Which word best describes the relationship between Marianna and her grandmother?

    a. Tense
    b. Distant
    c. Polite
    d. Loving

38. Which of the following is a statement of opinion?

    a. Grandmother made chicken with mole for the party
    b. Mariachi music was played at the party
    c. The food at the party was incredible
    d. Neighbors, friends, and family members attended the party

39. Where did Marianna go with her grandmother on the day of the party?

    a. To the open market
    b. To the beach
    c. To the ruins
    d. To the supermarket

40. According to the story, what is the main ingredient of chicle?

    a. Chicken
    b. Chocolate
    c. Sugar and spices
    d. Sapodilla pulp

Answers and Explanations

TEKS Standard §110.15(b)(6)

1. B: We learn in the sentence 1 that this story is set at Grandma's house. It refers to Grandma's sofa, and says Becca thinks her house is dull.

TEKS Standard §110.15(b)(3)(A)

2. A: When the story begins, Becca is extremely bored, because she thinks that life at Grandma's house is so uninteresting. However, by the end she has learned that there are many different ways to have fun. This is the main theme of the story.

TEKS Standard §110.15(b)(6)

3. D: At the beginning of the story, Becca is extremely bored.

TEKS Standard §110.15(b)(6)

4. C: Becca thinks that life at Grandma's house is "dull."

TEKS Standard §110.15(b)(6)(B)

5. B: When the story begins, Becca is extremely bored, because she thinks that life at Grandma's house is so uninteresting. However, by the end she has learned that there are many different ways to have fun.

TEKS Standard §110.15(b)(6)

6. C: Grandma says that when she was a child, she used to play outside.

TEKS Standard §110.15(b)(6)(C)

7. C: This story is written in third-person point of view. That means the story is told by someone who isn't in the story. If Becca or Grandma were telling the story, it would be in the first person. When you are talking or writing to someone, and you use their name or "you", you're using the second person.

TEKS Standard §110.15(b)(3)(A)

8. A: The author's main purpose in writing this story is to entertain the reader. It's true that the reader learns some information about life several decades ago, and that reading this story might make some kids change their minds about what's boring and what isn't, but those aren't the author's main reasons for writing the story.

TEKS Standard §110.15(b)(11)(B)

9. C: A fact is something that is true, no matter what anyone else thinks. An opinion is what someone thinks about something; other people may have a different opinion. The only statement of fact among these answer choices is that milk used to be delivered in glass bottles. The rest of the answer choices are all statements of opinion.

TEKS Standard §110.15(b)(6)

10. B: In sentence 24 we learn that Becca and Grandma ate lunch in a blanket fort they built.

TEKS Standard §110.15(b)(6)

11. D: In paragraph 8 Becca asked Grandma to get a computer.

TEKS Standard §110.15(b)(6)

12. B: Grandma has the more positive attitude in this story, and by the end of the story, she has helped Becca have a better attitude, too.

TEKS Standard §110.15(b)(6)

13. B: Paragraph 22 is the first paragraph to show the change in Becca's attitude, when she suggests that they play checkers. Earlier, she would have thought checkers was boring if Grandma had suggested it, but now she is eager to play.

TEKS Standard §110.15(b)(11)

14. C: Paragraph 1 says that it's estimated that there are over 300 Native American tribes. A, B, and D are not the best choices because they do not accurately represent the number of Native American tribes.

TEKS Standard §110.15(b)(11)

15. B: In paragraph 1, we learn that in Native American culture, dance is used to communicate many different kinds of messages.

TEKS Standard §110.15(b)(11)

16. A: The Iroquois corn husk dance and the Hopi Snake Ceremonial were both intended to bring good crops. The story says the Hopi used their dance for "a good harvest", which means a lot of crops for food.

TEKS Standard §110.15(b)(11)(B)

17. D: This is the only statement of fact. The rest of the answer choices are statements of opinion.

TEKS Standard §110.15(b)(11)

18. C: Paragraph 3 says that in many Native American tribes the eagle feather represents strength.

TEKS Standard §110.15(b)(3)

19. A: The author's main purpose in writing this article is to inform the reader about Native American dance.

TEKS Standard §110.15(b)(6)

20. B: Paragraph 1 indicates the narrator is of Cherokee heritage.

TEKS Standard §110.15(b)(6)(C)

21. A: This story is written in first person – that means that the person telling the story is part of the story.

TEKS Standard §110.15(b)(6)

22. D: Paragraph 1 indicates the narrator enjoys powwows because they represent the narrator's heritage.

TEKS Standard §110.15(b)(3)(A)

23. A: The main theme of this story is that Native American dancing tells a story. The author stresses this by closing with these words: "But although each dance was different, they all told a story. It was an ancient story: the story of my people."

TEKS Standard §110.15(b)(11)(B)

24. D is the only answer choice that represents an opinion. It's an opinion because one person might think that Native American dancing is emotionally powerful, but another person might disagree. A, B, and C are all factual statements.

TEKS Standard §110.15(b)(6)

25. B: The story says the narrator was looking at the items for sale on the tables before the dancing began.

TEKS Standard §110.15(b)(3)(A)

26. C: The importance of dancing in the Native American culture is a central theme in both stories.

TEKS Standard §110.15(b)(6) and (11)

27. A: Both stories compare Native American dancing to language, by saying that it tells a story, or communicates a message.

TEKS Standard §110.15(b)(6)

28. B: The Spanish word for grandmother is "abuela". The author tells us this by inserting "her grandmother" after "her grandmother", set off by dashes.

TEKS Standard §110.15(b)(6)

29. B: Paragraph 1 says this story is set in Tampico, Mexico.

TEKS Standard §110.15(b)(6)

30. A: We read in paragraph 7 that Marianna and her family visit Aztec ruins while on their trip.

TEKS Standard §110.15(b)(6)(A)

31. C most accurately completes the chart of Marianna's vacation. After the visit to the open market, Marianna goes to a big party at her abuela's house, which is right before she and her family leave for hom.

TEKS Standard §110.15(b)(6)

32. D: Paragraphs 8 through 11 discuss Marianna's visit with her cousins.

TEKS Standard §110.15(b)(6)

33. B: In paragraph 10, we learn that "futbol" means "soccer" in Spanish.

TEKS Standard §110.15(b)(6)

34. A: The author wrote from Marianna's point of view to show her thoughts and feelings to the reader.

TEKS Standard §110.15(b)(6)

35. C: Paragraph 13 shows Marianna does not want to go home because she loves Abuela and loves Mexico. A.

TEKS Standard §110.15(b)(8)

36. B: Paragraph 6 uses personification to describe the wind when it says "the gentle sea breeze kissed her face." Personification means talking about something that isn't human as if it is human. The breeze can't really kiss someone's face, but the author uses that figure of speech to help make the feeling of the breeze more realistic for the reader.

TEKS Standard §110.15(b)(6)(B)

37. D: Marianna and her grandmother clearly have a very loving relationship.

TEKS Standard §110.15(b)(11)(B)

38. C is the only statement of opinion. Marianna thought the food at the party was "incredible", but that's how she felt about it. Others may have felt differently about the food.

TEKS Standard §110.15(b)(6)

39. A: Marianna went to the open market with Abuela on the day of the party. This information can be found in paragraph 17.

TEKS Standard §110.15(b)(6)

40. D: is Paragraph 17 says chicle is made from sapodilla pulp.

How to Overcome Test Anxiety

Just the thought of taking a test is enough to make most people a little nervous. A test is an important event that can have a long-term impact on your future, so it's important to take it seriously and it's natural to feel anxious about performing well. But just because anxiety is normal, that doesn't mean that it's helpful in test taking, or that you should simply accept it as part of your life. Anxiety can have a variety of effects. These effects can be mild, like making you feel slightly nervous, or severe, like blocking your ability to focus or remember even a simple detail.

If you experience test anxiety—whether severe or mild—it's important to know how to beat it. To discover this, first you need to understand what causes test anxiety.

Causes of Test Anxiety

While we often think of anxiety as an uncontrollable emotional state, it can actually be caused by simple, practical things. One of the most common causes of test anxiety is that a person does not feel adequately prepared for their test. This feeling can be the result of many different issues such as poor study habits or lack of organization, but the most common culprit is time management. Starting to study too late, failing to organize your study time to cover all of the material, or being distracted while you study will mean that you're not well prepared for the test. This may lead to cramming the night before, which will cause you to be physically and mentally exhausted for the test. Poor time management also contributes to feelings of stress, fear, and hopelessness as you realize you are not well prepared but don't know what to do about it.

Other times, test anxiety is not related to your preparation for the test but comes from unresolved fear. This may be a past failure on a test, or poor performance on tests in general. It may come from comparing yourself to others who seem to be performing better or from the stress of living up to expectations. Anxiety may be driven by fears of the future—how failure on this test would affect your educational and career goals. These fears are often completely irrational, but they can still negatively impact your test performance.

> **Review Video: <u>3 Reasons You Have Test Anxiety</u>**
> Visit mometrix.com/academy and enter code: 428468

Elements of Test Anxiety

As mentioned earlier, test anxiety is considered to be an emotional state, but it has physical and mental components as well. Sometimes you may not even realize that you are suffering from test anxiety until you notice the physical symptoms. These can include trembling hands, rapid heartbeat, sweating, nausea, and tense muscles. Extreme anxiety may lead to fainting or vomiting. Obviously, any of these symptoms can have a negative impact on testing. It is important to recognize them as soon as they begin to occur so that you can address the problem before it damages your performance.

> **Review Video: 3 Ways to Tell You Have Test Anxiety**
> Visit mometrix.com/academy and enter code: 927847

The mental components of test anxiety include trouble focusing and inability to remember learned information. During a test, your mind is on high alert, which can help you recall information and stay focused for an extended period of time. However, anxiety interferes with your mind's natural processes, causing you to blank out, even on the questions you know well. The strain of testing during anxiety makes it difficult to stay focused, especially on a test that may take several hours. Extreme anxiety can take a huge mental toll, making it difficult not only to recall test information but even to understand the test questions or pull your thoughts together.

> **Review Video: How Test Anxiety Affects Memory**
> Visit mometrix.com/academy and enter code: 609003

Effects of Test Anxiety

Test anxiety is like a disease—if left untreated, it will get progressively worse. Anxiety leads to poor performance, and this reinforces the feelings of fear and failure, which in turn lead to poor performances on subsequent tests. It can grow from a mild nervousness to a crippling condition. If allowed to progress, test anxiety can have a big impact on your schooling, and consequently on your future.

Test anxiety can spread to other parts of your life. Anxiety on tests can become anxiety in any stressful situation, and blanking on a test can turn into panicking in a job situation. But fortunately, you don't have to let anxiety rule your testing and determine your grades. There are a number of relatively simple steps you can take to move past anxiety and function normally on a test and in the rest of life.

> **Review Video: How Test Anxiety Impacts Your Grades**
> Visit mometrix.com/academy and enter code: 939819

Physical Steps for Beating Test Anxiety

While test anxiety is a serious problem, the good news is that it can be overcome. It doesn't have to control your ability to think and remember information. While it may take time, you can begin taking steps today to beat anxiety.

Just as your first hint that you may be struggling with anxiety comes from the physical symptoms, the first step to treating it is also physical. Rest is crucial for having a clear, strong mind. If you are tired, it is much easier to give in to anxiety. But if you establish good sleep habits, your body and mind will be ready to perform optimally, without the strain of exhaustion. Additionally, sleeping well helps you to retain information better, so you're more likely to recall the answers when you see the test questions.

Getting good sleep means more than going to bed on time. It's important to allow your brain time to relax. Take study breaks from time to time so it doesn't get overworked, and don't study right before bed. Take time to rest your mind before trying to rest your body, or you may find it difficult to fall asleep.

> **Review Video: <u>The Importance of Sleep for Your Brain</u>**
> Visit mometrix.com/academy and enter code: 319338

Along with sleep, other aspects of physical health are important in preparing for a test. Good nutrition is vital for good brain function. Sugary foods and drinks may give a burst of energy but this burst is followed by a crash, both physically and emotionally. Instead, fuel your body with protein and vitamin-rich foods.

Also, drink plenty of water. Dehydration can lead to headaches and exhaustion, especially if your brain is already under stress from the rigors of the test. Particularly if your test is a long one, drink water during the breaks. And if possible, take an energy-boosting snack to eat between sections.

> **Review Video: <u>How Diet Can Affect your Mood</u>**
> Visit mometrix.com/academy and enter code: 624317

Along with sleep and diet, a third important part of physical health is exercise. Maintaining a steady workout schedule is helpful, but even taking 5-minute study breaks to walk can help get your blood pumping faster and clear your head. Exercise also releases endorphins, which contribute to a positive feeling and can help combat test anxiety.

When you nurture your physical health, you are also contributing to your mental health. If your body is healthy, your mind is much more likely to be healthy as well. So take time to rest, nourish your body with healthy food and water, and get moving as much as possible. Taking these physical steps will make you stronger and more able to take the mental steps necessary to overcome test anxiety.

> **Review Video: <u>How to Stay Healthy and Prevent Test Anxiety</u>**
> Visit mometrix.com/academy and enter code: 877894

Mental Steps for Beating Test Anxiety

Working on the mental side of test anxiety can be more challenging, but as with the physical side, there are clear steps you can take to overcome it. As mentioned earlier, test anxiety often stems from lack of preparation, so the obvious solution is to prepare for the test. Effective studying may be the most important weapon you have for beating test anxiety, but you can and should employ several other mental tools to combat fear.

First, boost your confidence by reminding yourself of past success—tests or projects that you aced. If you're putting as much effort into preparing for this test as you did for those, there's no reason you should expect to fail here. Work hard to prepare; then trust your preparation.

Second, surround yourself with encouraging people. It can be helpful to find a study group, but be sure that the people you're around will encourage a positive attitude. If you spend time with others who are anxious or cynical, this will only contribute to your own anxiety. Look for others who are motivated to study hard from a desire to succeed, not from a fear of failure.

Third, reward yourself. A test is physically and mentally tiring, even without anxiety, and it can be helpful to have something to look forward to. Plan an activity following the test, regardless of the outcome, such as going to a movie or getting ice cream.

When you are taking the test, if you find yourself beginning to feel anxious, remind yourself that you know the material. Visualize successfully completing the test. Then take a few deep, relaxing breaths and return to it. Work through the questions carefully but with confidence, knowing that you are capable of succeeding.

Developing a healthy mental approach to test taking will also aid in other areas of life. Test anxiety affects more than just the actual test—it can be damaging to your mental health and even contribute to depression. It's important to beat test anxiety before it becomes a problem for more than testing.

> **Review Video: Test Anxiety and Depression**
> Visit mometrix.com/academy and enter code: 904704

Study Strategy

Being prepared for the test is necessary to combat anxiety, but what does being prepared look like? You may study for hours on end and still not feel prepared. What you need is a strategy for test prep. The next few pages outline our recommended steps to help you plan out and conquer the challenge of preparation.

Step 1: Scope Out the Test

Learn everything you can about the format (multiple choice, essay, etc.) and what will be on the test. Gather any study materials, course outlines, or sample exams that may be available. Not only will this help you to prepare, but knowing what to expect can help to alleviate test anxiety.

Step 2: Map Out the Material

Look through the textbook or study guide and make note of how many chapters or sections it has. Then divide these over the time you have. For example, if a book has 15 chapters and you have five days to study, you need to cover three chapters each day. Even better, if you have the time, leave an extra day at the end for overall review after you have gone through the material in depth.

If time is limited, you may need to prioritize the material. Look through it and make note of which sections you think you already have a good grasp on, and which need review. While you are studying, skim quickly through the familiar sections and take more time on the challenging parts. Write out your plan so you don't get lost as you go. Having a written plan also helps you feel more in control of the study, so anxiety is less likely to arise from feeling overwhelmed at the amount to cover.

Step 3: Gather Your Tools

Decide what study method works best for you. Do you prefer to highlight in the book as you study and then go back over the highlighted portions? Or do you type out notes of the important information? Or is it helpful to make flashcards that you can carry with you? Assemble the pens, index cards, highlighters, post-it notes, and any other materials you may need so you won't be distracted by getting up to find things while you study.

If you're having a hard time retaining the information or organizing your notes, experiment with different methods. For example, try color-coding by subject with colored pens, highlighters, or post-it notes. If you learn better by hearing, try recording yourself reading your notes so you can listen while in the car, working out, or simply sitting at your desk. Ask a friend to quiz you from your flashcards, or try teaching someone the material to solidify it in your mind.

Step 4: Create Your Environment

It's important to avoid distractions while you study. This includes both the obvious distractions like visitors and the subtle distractions like an uncomfortable chair (or a too-comfortable couch that makes you want to fall asleep). Set up the best study environment possible: good lighting and a comfortable work area. If background music helps you focus, you may want to turn it on, but otherwise keep the room quiet. If you are using a computer to take notes, be sure you don't have any other windows open, especially applications like social media, games, or anything else that could distract you. Silence your phone and turn off notifications. Be sure to keep water close by so you stay hydrated while you study (but avoid unhealthy drinks and snacks).

Also, take into account the best time of day to study. Are you freshest first thing in the morning? Try to set aside some time then to work through the material. Is your mind clearer in the afternoon or evening? Schedule your study session then. Another method is to study at the same time of day that you will take the test, so that your brain gets used to working on the material at that time and will be ready to focus at test time.

Step 5: Study!

Once you have done all the study preparation, it's time to settle into the actual studying. Sit down, take a few moments to settle your mind so you can focus, and begin to follow your study plan. Don't give in to distractions or let yourself procrastinate. This is your time to prepare so you'll be ready to fearlessly approach the test. Make the most of the time and stay focused.

Of course, you don't want to burn out. If you study too long you may find that you're not retaining the information very well. Take regular study breaks. For example, taking five minutes out of every hour to walk briskly, breathing deeply and swinging your arms, can help your mind stay fresh.

As you get to the end of each chapter or section, it's a good idea to do a quick review. Remind yourself of what you learned and work on any difficult parts. When you feel that you've mastered the material, move on to the next part. At the end of your study session, briefly skim through your notes again.

But while review is helpful, cramming last minute is NOT. If at all possible, work ahead so that you won't need to fit all your study into the last day. Cramming overloads your brain with more information than it can process and retain, and your tired mind may struggle to recall even previously learned information when it is overwhelmed with last-minute study. Also, the urgent nature of cramming and the stress placed on your brain contribute to anxiety. You'll be more likely to go to the test feeling unprepared and having trouble thinking clearly.

So don't cram, and don't stay up late before the test, even just to review your notes at a leisurely pace. Your brain needs rest more than it needs to go over the information again. In fact, plan to finish your studies by noon or early afternoon the day before the test. Give your brain the rest of the day to relax or focus on other things, and get a good night's sleep. Then you will be fresh for the test and better able to recall what you've studied.

Step 6: Take a practice test

Many courses offer sample tests, either online or in the study materials. This is an excellent resource to check whether you have mastered the material, as well as to prepare for the test format and environment.

Check the test format ahead of time: the number of questions, the type (multiple choice, free response, etc.), and the time limit. Then create a plan for working through them. For example, if you have 30 minutes to take a 60-question test, your limit is 30 seconds per question. Spend less time on the questions you know well so that you can take more time on the difficult ones.

If you have time to take several practice tests, take the first one open book, with no time limit. Work through the questions at your own pace and make sure you fully understand them. Gradually work up to taking a test under test conditions: sit at a desk with all study materials put away and set a timer. Pace yourself to make sure you finish the test with time to spare and go back to check your answers if you have time.

After each test, check your answers. On the questions you missed, be sure you understand why you missed them. Did you misread the question (tests can use tricky wording)? Did you forget the information? Or was it something you hadn't learned? Go back and study any shaky areas that the practice tests reveal.

Taking these tests not only helps with your grade, but also aids in combating test anxiety. If you're already used to the test conditions, you're less likely to worry about it, and working through tests until you're scoring well gives you a confidence boost. Go through the practice tests until you feel comfortable, and then you can go into the test knowing that you're ready for it.

Test Tips

On test day, you should be confident, knowing that you've prepared well and are ready to answer the questions. But aside from preparation, there are several test day strategies you can employ to maximize your performance.

First, as stated before, get a good night's sleep the night before the test (and for several nights before that, if possible). Go into the test with a fresh, alert mind rather than staying up late to study.

Try not to change too much about your normal routine on the day of the test. It's important to eat a nutritious breakfast, but if you normally don't eat breakfast at all, consider eating just a protein bar. If you're a coffee drinker, go ahead and have your normal coffee. Just make sure you time it so that the caffeine doesn't wear off right in the middle of your test. Avoid sugary beverages, and drink enough water to stay hydrated but not so much that you need a restroom break 10 minutes into the test. If your test isn't first thing in the morning, consider going for a walk or doing a light workout before the test to get your blood flowing.

Allow yourself enough time to get ready, and leave for the test with plenty of time to spare so you won't have the anxiety of scrambling to arrive in time. Another reason to be early is to select a good seat. It's helpful to sit away from doors and windows, which can be distracting. Find a good seat, get out your supplies, and settle your mind before the test begins.

When the test begins, start by going over the instructions carefully, even if you already know what to expect. Make sure you avoid any careless mistakes by following the directions.

Then begin working through the questions, pacing yourself as you've practiced. If you're not sure on an answer, don't spend too much time on it, and don't let it shake your confidence. Either skip it and come back later, or eliminate as many wrong answers as possible and guess among the remaining ones. Don't dwell on these questions as you continue—put them out of your mind and focus on what lies ahead.

Be sure to read all of the answer choices, even if you're sure the first one is the right answer. Sometimes you'll find a better one if you keep reading. But don't second-guess yourself if you do immediately know the answer. Your gut instinct is usually right. Don't let test anxiety rob you of the information you know.

If you have time at the end of the test (and if the test format allows), go back and review your answers. Be cautious about changing any, since your first instinct tends to be correct, but make sure you didn't misread any of the questions or accidentally mark the wrong answer choice. Look over any you skipped and make an educated guess.

At the end, leave the test feeling confident. You've done your best, so don't waste time worrying about your performance or wishing you could change anything. Instead, celebrate the successful completion of this test. And finally, use this test to learn how to deal with anxiety even better next time.

Review Video: <u>5 Tips to Beat Test Anxiety</u>
Visit mometrix.com/academy and enter code: 570656

Important Qualification

Not all anxiety is created equal. If your test anxiety is causing major issues in your life beyond the classroom or testing center, or if you are experiencing troubling physical symptoms related to your anxiety, it may be a sign of a serious physiological or psychological condition. If this sounds like your situation, we strongly encourage you to seek professional help.

Thank You

We at Mometrix would like to extend our heartfelt thanks to you, our friend and patron, for allowing us to play a part in your journey. It is a privilege to serve people from all walks of life who are unified in their commitment to building the best future they can for themselves.

The preparation you devote to these important testing milestones may be the most valuable educational opportunity you have for making a real difference in your life. We encourage you to put your heart into it—that feeling of succeeding, overcoming, and yes, conquering will be well worth the hours you've invested.

We want to hear your story, your struggles and your successes, and if you see any opportunities for us to improve our materials so we can help others even more effectively in the future, please share that with us as well. **The team at Mometrix would be absolutely thrilled to hear from you!** So please, send us an email (support@mometrix.com) and let's stay in touch.

If you'd like some additional help, check out these other resources we offer for your exam:

http://MometrixFlashcards.com/STAAR

Additional Bonus Material

Due to our efforts to try to keep this book to a manageable length, we've created a link that will give you access to all of your additional bonus material.

Please visit https://www.mometrix.com/bonus948/staarg4read to access the information.